The Open University

Technology Foundation Course Unit 18

MODELLING II

Prepared by Michael Hussey
for the Technology Foundation Course Team

THE OPEN UNIVERSITY PRESS

The Technology Foundation Course Team

G. S. Holister (*Chairman and General Editor*)
K. Attenborough (*Engineering Mechanics*)
R. J. Beishon (*Systems*)
G. Bellis (*Scientific Officer*)
T. D. Bilham (*Course Assistant*)
D. A. Blackburn (*Materials Science*)
J. K. Cannell (*Engineering Mechanics*)
A. Clow (*BBC*)
G. P. Copp (*Assistant Editor*)
C. L. Crickmay (*Design*)
N. G. Cross (*Design*)
E. Goldwyn (*BBC*)
J. G. Gregory (*Editor*)
R. D. Harrison (*Educational Technology*)
R. Hermann (*Scientific Officer*)
M. J. L. Hussey (*Engineering Mechanics*)
A. B. Jolly (*BBC*)
J. C. Jones (*Design*)
L. M. Jones (*Systems*)
J. McCloy (*BBC*)
D. Nelson (*BBC*)
C. W. A. Newey (*Materials Science*)
S. Nicholson (*Design*)
G. Peters (*Systems*)
A. Porteous (*Engineering Mechanics*)
C. Robinson (*BBC*)
R. Roy (*Design*)
J. J. Sparkes (*Electronics*)
L. A. Suss (*Academic Administration*)
R. Thomas (*Economics*)
M. Weatherley (*BBC*)
G. H. Weaver (*Materials Science*)
P. I. Zorkoczy (*Electronics*)

The Open University Press
Walton Hall Bletchley Buckinghamshire

First published 1972

Copyright © 1972 The Open University

Produced in Great Britain by
Technical Filmsetters Europe Limited, 76 Great Bridgewater St, Manchester M1 5JY

SBN 335 02518 8

Open University courses provide a method of study for independent learners through an integrated teaching system, including text material, radio and television programmes and short residential courses. This text forms part of a series that makes up the correspondence element of the Technology Foundation Course.

The Open University's courses represent a new system of university-level education. Much of the teaching material is still in a developmental stage. Courses and course materials are, therefore, kept continually under revision. It is intended to issue regular up-dating notes as and when the need arises, and new editions will be brought out when necessary.

For general availability of supporting material referred to in this book, please write to the Director of Marketing, The Open University, Walton Hall, Bletchley, Buckinghamshire.

Further information on Open University courses may be obtained from the Admissions Office, The Open University, P.O. Box 48, Bletchley, Buckinghamshire.

Contents

Aims

The main aims of this unit are to explain two types of modelling technique (scale-modelling and mathematical programming) that are widely used in technology, to show the practical complications that can arise in their use and to bring out the difference in emphasis between the scientific and the technological use of models. After this the unit gives a very brief treatment of the 'model' of cost-benefit analysis, pointing out that there is no prototype against which the validity of such 'models' can be checked.

Objectives

After working through this unit you should be able to

(1) Explain what is meant by the dimensions of a physical quantity and by a dimensionless product.

* (2) Deduce the dimensions of a given quantity from its definition.

(3) Explain what is meant by a consistent system of units of measurement.

(4) Check a supposed physical relationship for dimensional consistency.

* (5) Explain the conditions that must be satisfied before a scale model can be used to predict the behaviour of a prototype.

(6) Explain how incompatible scaling relationships can be implied when a scale model is to be made, exemplify ways of getting round such difficulties, and note some precautions that must be observed in such cases.

* (7) Use a graphical method to find the maximum or minimum value of a linear objective-function of two design variables when there are constraints in the form of linear inequalities on the values the design variables can assume.

* (8) Explain by means of sketches the problems of optimization when the objective-function and constraints are non-linear and hence explain what is meant by a sub-optimum.

* (9) Explain the difference between the 'model' of cost-benefit analysis and other models used in technology.

* (10) Explain the difference between absolute conditions and financial penalties as they affect optimization procedures.

What you have to do

The most essential parts of this unit are Sections 2.1, 3.3, 4.5, and the appendix. The remainder requires some algebra. If you can follow the notation, you will find it revealing, but it may be omitted without prejudice to the remainder of the course. There are two exercises in Section 2.2.7 and three in Section 3.1, and the 7 SAQs are all on Sections 2 and 3. One SAQ will probably take about an hour and should be omitted unless you have plenty of time, but consult the solution given. You will need graph paper for some of these. The TV programme deals with the investigation of wind-induced 'galloping' of snow-laden power lines, which was tackled using a number of modelling techniques. The cassette illustrates the use of scale models in designing auditoria and relates directly to Section 2.1.

* Questions based on these objectives may be set in the examination.

Section 1

Introduction

In Modelling I we first dealt with the general ideas of modelling and then attended particularly to the ways in which mathematics and science are related to technology through the assistance they offer the technologist in his use of models. Mathematics, we saw, provides a highly developed language for modelling, while science offers a huge range of ready-made models which the technologist can use as and when he has need of them.

In this unit we shall look first at applications of modelling in two fields of endeavour that are more characteristically technological—the fields of scale-modelling and of operational research. We shall then consider briefly what is distinctive about the technologist's use of models, and finally we shall look at the way in which technological progress is promoted or constrained by the availability or unavailability of good models.

Scale models

2.1 An introductory example

Very large costs are involved in the construction of a concert hall, and the success of the project is critically dependent on the listening qualities of the auditorium. These qualities depend in a complicated manner on the shape and size of the auditorium and on the ways in which the energy of sound waves is absorbed during their passage through the air and in their reflections from the various surfaces they encounter.

A listener at any one particular position in the auditorium hears not only the sounds that travel straight to him from the orchestra but in addition the innumerable dying echoes of these sounds that result from their many reflections. A staccato sound is thus heard to die away through a succession of echoes, a phenomenon called reverberation. The extent of reverberation is an important determinant of the acoustic suitability of an auditorium. The requirements of a concert hall are different in this respect from those of, say, a lecture theatre, or, again, of a cathedral.

A further matter of importance is that the sound produced by the orchestra should be distributed as evenly as possible throughout the auditorium.

The complexity of these acoustic problems defies the use of a mathematical model, but a scale model can be used to assess the prospective listening qualities of an auditorium before too great a commitment to a particular design is assumed.

The use of a scale model begins with the construction of a scaled-down auditorium with all lengths say $\frac{1}{K}$ times those in the proposed concert hall. The need for scaled-down orchestras and listeners is by-passed by the use of small loudspeakers in place of the former and small microphones, disposed about the auditorium, in place of the latter. The path of any echo that can be heard at a given point in the full-scale auditorium is thus automatically reproduced in the model. It remains to ensure that the various sound-absorbing properties of the surfaces and of the air in the model are appropriately arranged and that reverberations in the model give proper guidance as to the reverberations to be expected in the prototype.

When we consider the matter of reverberation in the model we find the necessity for a further kind of scaling. The succession of echoes that make up the reverberation of a staccato sound are spread out in time because while the various paths they follow are of different lengths the speed with which the sound-waves travel is the same for all paths. The lapse of time between the arrivals of any two of the echoes is equal to the difference in lengths of their paths divided by the speed of sound. Now, in the model all lengths are reduced as compared with those in the prototype, but the speed of sound is the same in both the model and the prototype. The lapse of time between the arrivals of the two echoes in the model will therefore be smaller than for corresponding echoes in the full-sized auditorium by a factor equal to the scale of lengths, $\frac{1}{K}$; reverberations in the model will thus be compressed in time. The significance of reverberation in a musical context relates to the way in which the echoes of one note die away while merging with the next note. If the appropriate effect is to be created in the model, where sounds die away more quickly than in the prototype, it follows that the notes must succeed each other more rapidly in the model—in fact K times as quickly as in the real auditorium. One second in time for the model must hence represent K seconds in the prototype and the scale $\frac{1}{K}$, chosen for lengths must also be adopted for time. The alternative, that of arranging for a reduced speed of sound in the model, is not practicable.

The procedure of testing thus involves several steps. The first is the recording of a piece of music in the absence of reverberation. This is done in a specially designed room called an anechoic chamber, whose size and finishes are so arranged as to eliminate all echoes. The second step is to copy the first recording to produce a version K times as fast. Next this rapid version of the recording is played through the loudspeaker in the model and the effects recorded from the various microphones in the model auditorium. Finally these last recordings are reproduced at a speed equal to that of the orchestra's original performance. Provided that the sound-absorbing properties of the model have been properly contrived, these last recordings will reveal the listening quality at those positions in the real concert-hall that correspond to the placings of the microphones in the model.

To get the right measure of sound-absorption in the model requires attention to two essentially different phenomena. The first is the attenuation of sound in its passage through the air, and the second the reduction in their energy that occurs when sound waves are reflected from surfaces.

The absorption of energy from sound waves by the air is gauged by the fraction of its energy that a wave loses in travelling a unit distance. If corresponding waves are to lose the same fraction of energy in following corresponding paths in both model and prototype, then because the path in the model is shorter by a factor $\frac{1}{K}$, the fractional rate of absorption per unit distance must be made greater in the model by the factor K. This is possible in consequence of a fortunate coincidence. The time-scale for the model is, as we have seen, compressed, so the frequencies of sounds in the model are K times as great as in the prototype. It happens that sounds of these higher frequencies are more strongly absorbed in air than sounds of ordinary musical frequencies. Indeed the increase of frequencies by a factor K produces an increase of absorption by a factor greater than K. This disproportionate increase can, however, be offset by reducing the humidity of the air because the sound-absorbing propensity of moist air decreases with falling humidity. (Because this process of compensation is not quite perfect there is a practical restriction on the scale of acoustic models: $\frac{1}{K}$ cannot be made less than about $\frac{1}{12}$, so acoustic models cannot be made very small).

The absorption of sound by a surface depends both on the material and nature of the surface and on the frequency of the sound. In general, therefore, because the frequencies in the model differ from those in the prototype the materials used in the model have to differ from those in the prototype. The selection of appropriate materials is a matter for experiment. The relevant experiments involve the use of another special room and an acoustic model of it to the chosen scale, $\frac{1}{K}$. This room is designed, in contrast to the anechoic chamber, to provide strong reverberation. An area of the wall-surface of the full-scale room is covered with the surfacing material that is to be modelled, and the corresponding area in the model reverberation room covered with a material that, it is thought, may be suitable for use in the model. Recordings made in the reverberation room are compared with those produced, by the methods of acoustic modelling, from the model of the room. In this way various modelling materials can be tested and satisfactory ones chosen. Thus, for example, certain kinds of velvet are found to be suitable for imitating carpets.

In a real auditorium the seats and the audience constitute important sound-absorbers. Again a reverberation room and its acoustic model can be used to find suitable simulacra. It has been found that figures cut from a rigid polyurethane foam and provided with sanded pine heads (!) satisfactorily model members of the audience. The irregular surface of the cut plastic foam absorbs the high-frequency sound in the model in a way that corresponds well with the effects of clothing at ordinary musical frequencies.

Your audio cassette for this unit will enable you to judge for yourself as to the success of acoustic modelling.

2.2 General considerations in scale modelling

The example of acoustic modelling brings out some important points about scale-modelling in general. The first point concerns the sort of problem in whose solution scale-modelling is likely to be helpful. In the matter of acoustics the various phenomena that are of dominant importance are well understood in a piecemeal way—the generation, propagation, reflection, absorption and reception of sound-waves. The relevant elements of the model are thus fairly easy to enumerate (you may find it useful here to refer back to Figure 1 of Modelling I). They are the shape of the auditorium, the position from which the sound emanates, the positions at which it is to be received, the positions and acoustic properties of the surfaces from which the sounds can be reflected, the absorptive capacity of the air, and the frequencies of the sounds themselves.

Thus the question as to *what* contributes to the emergent property of listening quality is settled. The really difficult and intricate question is 'How?' or, 'What are the relevant interactions?'

However, the technologist's interest is in the outcome of these interactions—the emergent behaviour—and if this can be assessed without a comprehensive description of the interactions he will be quite satisfied. In the use of a scale model the essential idea is that whatever the interactions in the prototype may be the physical behaviour of the model will reproduce these interactions automatically because the same sort of thing will go on in both the model and the prototype. As long as we know *what* matters, we do not *have* to know exactly *why* or *how*. Of course we are unlikely to guess correctly what does matter unless we have at least a vague idea as to why it matters or how it could matter, but we do not need a very detailed understanding of these things. A problem of the kind in which a scale model may be of help is thus one in which the essential elements contributing to the behaviour of interest are fairly easily perceived but their interactions are extremely complicated. Many problems of this sort are encountered in those fields of engineering that have to do with fluids—that is with liquids and gases. Consequently scale models are often used in studies for the design of pumps and turbines, ships and aeroplanes, harbours and coastal protection schemes, and for problems concerning the movement of silt in rivers and estuaries and the dissipation of waste heat from power stations. Some engineering models are shown in Figures 1–5.

A second point raised by the example of acoustic modelling is that quantities other than length may have to be scaled—in the example it was necessary to use a compressed scale of time for the model—and that the choice of scales for different quantities is not a completely free choice.

8

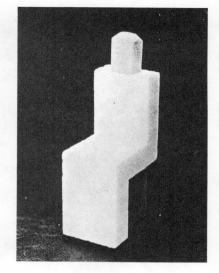

Figure 1   Model audience for testing the acoustic properties of an auditorium. (J. Hegvold and Applied Acoustics.)

Figure 2   Wind-tunnel model of Concorde. (B.A.C. Ltd.)

Figure 3   Oil tankers are nowadays built so large that many ports cannot accommodate them. One solution is to moor them to a fixed tower or floating buoy positioned outside the port and to pump the oil ashore from there. In this model a supertanker is being subjected to variable winds, waves and currents, and the forces on the buoy are being determined. (Hydraulics Research Station, Wallingford, England.)

Figure 4   Models can provide much useful information on flood levels and flood alleviation schemes. This 1/300 model of part of the River Trent in England reproduced both the river channel and the bordering flood plains. It was constructed to examine the effects of a motorway viaduct on flooding in the valley. (Hydraulics Research Station, Wallingford, England.)

Figure 5   As the factors affecting the stability of beaches are many and complex, it is often impracticable to study the behaviour of beaches in nature. In models, however, the various factors can be controlled and their effects isolated. In these studies of the effects of groynes on sandy and shingle beaches, waves, tides and tidal currents can be reproduced and varied within a wide range. (Hydraulics Research Station, Wallingford, England.)

Once the scale of length was chosen for the acoustic model quite definite scales for time and for the absorptive capacity of the air were implied. The relationship between these scaling factors was argued out from the details of the problem, but there is a general approach to these questions of scales. We will go on now to examine this general approach, leaving the other points illustrated by the example of acoustic modelling to be taken up from time to time.

2.2.1   Units of measurement

You are probably used to judging distances in inches, feet, yards and miles. If you ask a question like, 'How far is it from the pub to the bus stop?' you expect an answer that specifies some number of one of these standard units of length. The number is called the *measure* of the length in question, in the stated units. If you were asked what a yard was you might answer 'three feet'. Asked what a foot was you might then answer 'twelve inches'. However, if this line of questioning were to be continued you would have, eventually, to point to something and say, 'That is a yard long', or something of that sort. There is nothing absolute about the units we use for measuring things; they are defined by agreement. The Imperial Standard Yard was the distance between two lines on gold plugs sunk into a particular bar of bronze alloy when the bar was supported in a carefully defined way under specified conditions of atmospheric pressure and temperature.

In 1951 the yard was redefined as 0.9144 metre—the standard bar was then known to be shortening at a rate of more than one millionth of an inch a year (while remaining, of course, 36 inches long by definition) and redefinition was vital for precision engineering. The metre is now defined in terms of the wavelength of light from a particular kind of lamp.

The metre is thus nowadays the primary unit of length. It is one of the primary units in the Système International d'Unités. There are six other primary SI units, of which the ones that we will be most concerned with here are the kilogramme and the second, used respectively for the measurement of mass and of time. The subject of mechanics requires no primary units besides those of mass, length and time. All the other units needed, for example, in the measurement of areas, volumes, velocities, forces, etc., can be derived from these primary ones; they are called *derived units*.

An idea that is useful in dealing with derived units is that of the *dimensions* of a physical quantity. In the SI system the primary units for mechanics are those of mass, length and time. These are quite independent. There is no way in which a length could be expressed in the units of mass or of time. We say that masses, lengths and times are of different dimensions. This use of the word 'dimension' has nothing to do with size, it is more in line with the popular expression 'He will have to add a new dimension to his thinking'. Indeed, if we are to extend our interest into the realms of thermodynamics we do actually have to add a further dimension. By adding a primary unit of temperature—the Kelvin in the Système International— we introduce the independent dimension of temperature. It is not essential for the primary units and fundamental dimensions to relate to the same physical quantities. For example, the Système International is extended to electro-magnetic phenomena by the primary unit of electric current— the ampere, but electric charge is often preferred to electric current as a fundamental dimension.

We can represent the dimension of mass by $[M]$, that of length by $[L]$ and that of time by $[T]$. In this notation M, for example, need not stand for any particular mass. All masses have the dimension of mass. Thus when square brackets are placed round the symbol for a physical quantity the resulting compound symbol means 'the dimensions of the enclosed quantity'. Inside the square brackets, therefore, any one mass is as good as any other, and there is no point in distinguishing them.

It is now easy to express the dimensions of physical quantities other than masses, lengths and times in terms of the fundamental dimensions, $[M]$, $[L]$, and $[T]$. For example, a rectangle with sides of lengths l_1 and l_2 has an area, A, given by

$$A = l_1 l_2$$

and each side of the equation must have the dimensions of area. So we can write

$$[A] = [l_1 l_2] = [LL] = [L^2]$$

and say 'the dimensions of area are $[L^2]$'. In changing each of l_1 and l_2 into L we are using the idea that inside the brackets one length is as good as any other.

As another example consider density. Density is defined as mass per unit volume. A volume, since it is calculated as the product of three lengths, has the dimensions $[L^3]$. Hence, if ρ is a density,

$$[\rho] = \frac{[M]}{[L^3]} = [M/L^3] = [ML^{-3}].$$

The dimensions of every sort of physical quantity encountered in mechanics can be expressed as $[M^p L^q T^r]$ by some choice of the powers p, q, and r. The appropriate values can be found from the definition of the quantity, as we just saw in the cases of area, volume and density. As one more example, Newton's second law of motion defines a force, F, in terms of the acceleration, a, produced in a mass M. The law is written

$$F = Ma$$

hence

$$\begin{aligned} F &= [M][a] \\ &= [M][L/T^2] \\ &= [MLT^{-2}]. \end{aligned}$$

In this derivation I have used $[L/T^2]$ as the dimensions of acceleration in anticipation of the following exercise.

Exercises

(a) Use the definition of a uniform velocity to find the dimensions of velocity, V, in terms of $[M]$, $[L]$, and $[T]$.

(b) Use the definition of a uniform acceleration, a, to find the dimensions of acceleration.

Table 1 lists some physical quantities of significance in the mechanics of fluids. It shows their dimensions in terms of $[M]$, $[L]$ and $[T]$ and, in addition, their derived SI units of measurement. You can see that these units are derived from the dimensional expressions simply by replacing $[M]$ by kg, $[L]$ by m, and $[T]$ by s. A system of units derived in this way from a set of primary units is called a consistent system. Within a consistent system of units there are no arbitrary conversion factors such as $5\,280\,\text{ft} = 1$ mile. For convenience certain derived units may be given names, as is remarked in column 5 of Table 1. This does not change their status as derived units.

(a) The uniform velocity of a body is the distance it travels in a given time divided by that time. The distance is of dimension $[L]$ and the time of dimension $[T]$. The dimensions of velocity are therefore

$$[V] = [L]/[T] = [L/T] = [LT^{-1}].$$

(b) If a body accelerates uniformly from rest, its acceleration is found by dividing its velocity at any instant by the time for which it has been moving. Hence

$$[a] = \frac{[V]}{[T]} = [LT^{-1}/T] = [LT^{-2}].$$

Table 1

Physical Quantity	Symbol	Dimensions	SI units	Remarks
mass	M	$[M]$	kg	Fundamental dimensions and primary units
length	L	$[L]$	m	
time	T	$[T]$	s	
angle	α	$[M^0L^0T^0]$	radians (rad)	A *dimensionless* quantity
area	A	$[L^2]$	m^2	
volume	v	$[L^3]$	m^3	
velocity	V	$[LT^{-1}]$	m s^{-1}	
acceleration	a	$[LT^{-2}]$	m s^{-2}	Derived dimensions and units
density	ρ	$[ML^{-3}]$	kg m^{-3}	
force	F	$[MLT^{-2}]$	kg m s^{-2}	The SI unit of force is named the newton N
*viscosity	μ	$[ML^{-1}T^{-1}]$	kg m^{-1} s^{-1}	
†bulk modulus	K	$[ML^{-1}T^{-2}]$	kg m^{-1} s^{-2}	
‡surface tension	σ	$[MT^{-2}]$	kg s^{-2}	

* Viscosity is the property of a fluid that characterizes its reluctance to flow. Golden syrup is a very viscous liquid.

† The bulk modulus of a fluid characterizes its resistance to compression. Liquids generally have much greater bulk moduli than do gases.

‡ The pressure inside a bubble is slightly greater than that outside. It is contained by a tension in the skin of the bubble. Every liquid surface exerts a surface-tension of this kind—which is why droplets of liquid do not spread out into indefinitely thin layers on a solid surface.

There is no particular reason for choosing $[M]$, $[L]$, and $[T]$ as fundamental dimensions. Certain consistent systems of units have been based on the dimensions of force, length and time: $[F]$, $[L]$ and $[T]$. In these systems the dimensions of mass, as found from Newton's second law of motion, are

$$[M] = [FL^{-1}T^2].$$

(In the subject of statics time plays no part; all the quantities relevant to statics have dimensions expressible in terms of $[F]$ and $[L]$ alone.) This does not imply a need for a primary unit of force to replace the primary unit of mass. As I remarked earlier, in the Système International the primary unit of electric current is the ampere. The dimensions of electric current are nevertheless usually taken to be $[QT^{-1}]$ where $[Q]$, the dimension of electric charge, is taken as a fundamental dimension. The fundamental dimensions need not be those of the primary units.

In talking of modelling in the mechanics of fluids it is helpful to consider a system of dimensions based on those of length, velocity and density. The fundamental dimensions are then $[L]$, $[V]$, and $[\rho]$. Mass and time have the derived dimensions $[M] = [\rho L^3]$ and $[T] = [LV^{-1}]$. This choice replaces the dimensions of Table 1 with those of Table 2.*

2.2.2 Descriptions without dimensions

As I remarked at the beginning of the last section, we state physical quantities by giving a number (the *measure* of the quantity) and a unit of measurement. We could express the width of this page, say, as 8.25 in. or as 21.0 cm. You see that the measure changes when the unit of measurement is changed. In contrast, the ratio of the height of the page to its width does not depend upon the units in which the height and the width are measured—provided both measurements are made within the same system of units. This ratio is that of a length to a length; its dimensions are thus $[L]/[L] = [LL^{-1}] = [L^0]$; we say that it is dimensionless. Angles are also dimensionless, as you can see from Tables 1 and 2.

Table 2 Dimensions based on those of length, velocity and density

Physical Quantity	Symbol	Dimensions
length	L	$[L]$
velocity	V	$[V]$
density	ρ	$[\rho]$
angle	α	$[L^0 V^0 \rho^0]$
area	A	$[L^2]$
volume	v	$[L^3]$
mass	M	$[\rho L^3]$
time	T	$[LV^{-1}]$
acceleration	a	$[V^2 L^{-1}]$
force	F	$[\rho V^2 L^2]$
viscosity	μ	$[\rho V L]$
bulk modulus	K	$[\rho V^2]$
surface tension	σ	$[\rho V^2 L]$

The physical behaviour of things cannot be supposed to depend upon our arbitrary choice of units of measurement. We may, therefore, expect that the physical relationships between the various quantities entering into the description of a phenomenon must be expressible in a dimensionless way. Let us look at a characteristic problem in fluid mechanics and see how it may be given a description in dimension-free terms.

Consider, then, a ship sailing on a boundless, bottomless ocean. (These absurd suppositions are indirect ways of saying that for the purposes of our modelling exercise we are regarding the ship as sufficiently distant from any jetty and in sufficiently deep water for its distance offshore and the depth of water to be irrelevant.) We can describe the shape of the ship, the depth to which it is immersed, the height of the bow-wave, the height of the barnacles on the hull, indeed all lengths of interest (say, L_1, L_2, L_3, L_4, L_5, and so on) by stating not their measures in any particular system of units but the ratios they bear to the length of the ship. (I have chosen the length arbitrarily—it could have been the beam.) As ratios between

---

* The units of measurement are still the SI units. They could be obtained from the dimensional expressions of Table 2 by replacing $[L]$ by m, $[V]$ by m s^{-1}, $[\rho]$ by kg m^{-3}.

lengths these are all dimensionless quantities. The length of the ship itself will be expressed as the ratio 1 which it bears to itself. We can note the actual length, L_0, of the ship in some system of units for later reference and pass on to velocities.

The velocities (say V_1, V_2, V_3, etc.) that may concern us certainly include the forward velocity of the ship relative to very distant still water and might extend, say, to the velocities of the waves created by the ship's passage. Again we can choose a velocity of reference—the forward velocity of the ship is the obvious choice—and describe all other velocities by the ratios they bear to it. The reference velocity is now characterized by the ratio 1 that it bears to itself. We can note the actual value, V_0, of this velocity in our chosen system of units and proceed to densities.

To deal with densities (say, ρ_1, ρ_2, ρ_3, etc.) we again choose one for reference, describe all others by their ratios to it, and note the value, ρ_0, of our reference density in our chosen system of units.

Clearly we can continue this process through every kind of quantity, expressing all forces, for example, by the ratios they bear to a chosen reference force, all accelerations by their ratios to a reference acceleration, and so on. In this way we can pass from a description of the situation in the form represented in Figure 6(a) to that represented in Figure 6(b).

Figure 6   Getting the dimensions out of the description of a problem.

Nature of Quantity	Relevant Variables Appearing in Description					
Lengths	L_1	L_2	L_3	L_4	L_5	....
Velocities	V_1	V_2	V_3	V_4	V_5	....
Densities	ρ_1	ρ_2	ρ_3	ρ_4	ρ_5	....
Forces	F_1	F_2	F_3	F_4	F_5	....
Accelerations	a_1	a_2	a_3	a_4	a_5	....
Viscosities	μ_1	μ_2	μ_3	μ_4	μ_5	....
Times	T_1	T_2	T_3	T_4	T_5	....

Figure 6a

Nature of Quantity	Reference Quantity	Relevant Variables Appearing in Description					
Lengths	$L_1 \longrightarrow L_0$	1	L_2/L_1	L_3/L_1	L_4/L_1	L_5/L_1	....
Velocities	$V_1 \longrightarrow V_0$	1	V_2/V_1	V_3/V_1	V_4/V_1	V_5/V_1	....
Densities	$\rho_1 \longrightarrow \rho_0$	1	ρ_2/ρ_1	ρ_3/ρ_1	ρ_4/ρ_1	ρ_5/ρ_1	....
Forces	$F_1 \longrightarrow F_0$	1	F_2/F_1	F_3/F_1	F_4/F_1	F_5/F_1	....
Accelerations	$a_1 \longrightarrow a_0$	1	a_2/a_1	a_3/a_1	a_4/a_1	a_5/a_1	....
Viscosities	$\mu_1 \longrightarrow \mu_0$	1	μ_2/μ_1	μ_3/μ_1	μ_4/μ_1	μ_5/μ_1	....
Times	$T_1 \longrightarrow T_0$	1	T_2/T_1	T_3/T_1	T_4/T_1	T_5/T_1	....

Figure 6b

Nature of Quantity	Reference Quantity	Relevant Variables Appearing in Description					
Lengths	L_0	1	L_2/L_1	L_3/L_1	L_4/L_1	L_5/L_1	....
Velocities	V_0	1	V_2/V_1	V_3/V_1	V_4/V_1	V_5/V_1	....
Densities	ρ_0	1	ρ_2/ρ_1	ρ_3/ρ_1	ρ_4/ρ_1	ρ_5/ρ_1	....
Forces	$F_0/(\rho_0 L_0^2 V_0^2)$	1	F_2/F_1	F_3/F_1	F_4/F_1	F_5/F_1	....
Accelerations	$a_0 L_0/V_0^2$	1	a_2/a_1	a_3/a_1	a_4/a_1	a_5/a_1	....
Viscosities	$\mu_0/(\rho_0 L_0 V_0)$	1	μ_2/μ_1	μ_3/μ_1	μ_4/μ_1	μ_5/μ_1	....
Times	$(T_0 V_0/L_0)$	1	T_2/T_1	T_3/T_1	T_4/T_1	T_5/T_1	....

This description consists in sets of length ratios, velocity ratios, density ratios, force ratios and so on—all dimensionless—and a list of reference quantities, L_0, V_0, ρ_0, F_0, etc. The red boxes in Figures 6(a) and 6(b) enclose those quantities needing a system of units for their description.

Now we can go further still. By consulting Table 2 we find that the dimensions of force are $[\rho L^2 V^2]$, which implies that by multiplying together our reference density, the square of our reference velocity and the square of our reference length we obtain a quantity, $\rho_0 L_0^2 V_0^2$, with the dimensions of force. We can therefore characterize F_0, our previous reference force, by the ratio it bears to this quantity, that is, by $F_0/(\rho_0 V_0^2 L_0^2)$, which is dimensionless.

Exercise

If a_0 is the reference acceleration and L_0, V_0 and ρ_0 are the reference length, reference velocity and reference density, what would be a suitable dimensionless quantity by which to characterize a_0?

From Table 2 the dimensions of acceleration are $[V^2 L^{-1}]$. Hence V_0^2/L_0 has the dimensions of acceleration and $a_0/(V_0^2/L_0)$, i.e. $a_0 L_0/V_0^2$ is a dimensionless quantity suitable to characterize a_0.

Using this procedure, we are able to arrive at a description of the phenomenon that is shown in Figure 6(c), in which only three quantities, L_0, V_0, and ρ_0, remain in the dimensional form of description.

In setting out the arrays of Figure 6 I have not intended to imply that in the case of the ship, from which we started, we will actually be concerned with many different viscosities or densities, for example. I have given a general account of a procedure that can always be followed. It might happen that we were faced with a problem in which density was unlikely to be a relevant variable. In that case, we could possibly use $[L]$, $[V]$, and $[F]$ to recast Table 2. There is always some set of quantities that we can take to provide a set of fundamental dimensions and to serve us as $[L]$, $[V]$, and $[\rho]$ did in the above account. In statics, for example, as I mentioned before, $[L]$ and $[F]$ are suitable, and no other independent fundamental dimension is needed or can be found.

2.2.3 Buckingham's theorem

We have now seen that all the physical quantities relating to the sailing of a ship can be described in the manner of Figure 6(c). But our real interest in approaching this matter is in the relationships between these quantities. Now these relationships cannot depend essentially on our choice of a system of units of measurement. Our decision to measure lengths in metres rather than in cubits cannot possibly influence the way a ship moves through the water. So any expression of physical relationships must be unchanged when we change our units of measurement. The dimensionless ratios in Figure 6(c) do not change when we change units, but the measures of L_0, V_0 and ρ_0 do. Moreover, there is no way of putting L_0, V_0 and ρ_0 together to produce a dimensionless ratio—their dimensions are independent. We conclude that the relationships we are looking for do not involve L_0, V_0 or ρ_0 except where these occur in dimensionless combinations with other variables. Hence anything that is to be said about such relationships, for our ship or any other physical phenomena, can be said entirely in a language of dimensionless ratios.

The use of dimensionless ratios in the description of a problem has several advantages. The most obvious is the freedom from arbitrary systems of units. Another is a reduction in the number of variables appearing in the problem. If you look again at Figure 6 you will see that the variables that occupied one complete column of Figure 6(a) have been replaced, in Figure 6(c), by 1s, which are in no way variable. In Figure 6(c) though, new variables have appeared in the previous column, but L_0, V_0 and ρ_0, as we just saw, can be forgotten. The total number of variables that matters in the final description is therefore less by three, in this case, than the number in the first description. The number three is, of course, the number of independent dimensions in the original description of the problem.

The conclusions drawn in this section constitute Buckingham's theorem of dimensional analysis, which can be stated as follows. Relationships between the variables describing a physical phenomenon can all be expressed in terms of dimensionless products or ratios. The number of such dimensionless quantities will be the total number of variables concerned in the problem less the number of independent dimensions essentially involved.

2.2.4 Similarity

With Buckingham's theorem in mind we can easily imagine a situation in which, for example, there are two different ships of different lengths sailing at different speeds on different oceans, for which nevertheless all relevant *dimensionless* data, as set out in arrays like Figure 6(c) coincide. This suggests that measurements could be made on one of them in order to find out about the other one—which is, of course, the underlying idea of scale modelling. When we attempt to achieve such a correspondence between a model and its prototype we say we are trying to establish *similarity* between them.

In general we cannot exert direct control over all the dimensionless quantities characterizing a model—our very purpose in building the model is to use it to *find* the values of some of them. In approaching any problem, however, we are aware of a distinction between two sorts of variables—the independent variables and the dependent variables. The independent variables are the ones that are *fixed* in the posing of the problem (they are the relevant elementary properties, in the terminology of Figure 1 of Modelling 1); the dependent variables are what we look upon as consequences of the independent ones (they constitute the emergent properties, or behaviour). We need only proceed, as in the example of acoustic modelling, by establishing similarity with regard to the independent variables; the others look after themselves, through the very relationships about which the model can enlighten us.

It is important to realise that Buckingham's theorem does NOT tell us that it is *possible* to match all relevant dimensionless quantities in the prototype and a model. It merely suggests that we can try. It is not actually about physics at all—it is about the sort of mathematics that can be applied to physics.

2.2.5 Some types of similarity

If we succeed in matching the values of all the length-ratios (the dimensionless quantities in the first row of Figure 6 (c)) for a model to those of its prototype we say that we have produced *geometric similarity*. Geometrically similar things have their shape in common; they are of the same proportions and angles between their corresponding parts are identical (see Figure 7). The scale of the model (which we should, more exactly, call the scale of length) is given by the ratio of the reference length, $L_{0(m)}$, for the model to that, $L_{0(p)}$, for the prototype—that is, the ratio $L_{0(m)}/L_{0(p)}$. The same ratio subsists between any pair of corresponding lengths, one in the model and the other in the prototype.

If the model and the prototype are geometrically similar and also happen to match in all their velocity-ratios (as listed in the second row of Figure 6(c)) they are said to possess *kinematic similarity*.

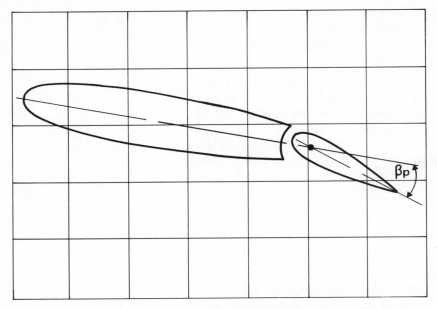
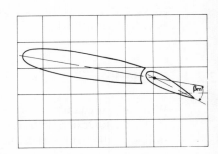

Figure 7   Geometrical similarity. Each of these drawings shows the cross-section of an aircraft's wing. The figures are drawn in exactly corresponding ways over grids of small squares. The proportions of the two sections are identical, and so are the aileron angles β_m and β_p.

If the matching extends beyond that needed for geometric and kinematic similarity to include the identity of force-ratios (the fourth row of dimensionless quantities in Figure 6(c)) the model and prototype are said to have *dynamic similarity*. The requirements for dynamic similarity automatically include the matching of density-ratios but are more comprehensive in that forces due to friction, elasticity, surface-tension and so on must also be taken into account.

The consideration of scales is more complicated for kinematic and dynamic similarity than for geometric similarity.

2.2.6   Scales

If scales of length and of velocity are fixed for a model that is kinematically similar to its prototype, the scale of time is automatically implied, as we argued in an *ad hoc* way in the example of acoustic modelling. The systematic approach to the interdependence of the scales of length, velocity and time hinges on the matching of dimensionless ratios between the prototype and the model. The dimensionless quantity characterizing reference times is shown in the seventh row of Figure 6(c) to be $\dfrac{T_0 V_0}{L_0}$ (sometimes called the Thomson number). If this number is to have the same value in both model and prototype, then

$$\frac{T_{0(m)}V_{0(m)}}{L_{0(m)}} = \frac{T_{0(p)}V_{0(p)}}{L_{0(p)}}$$

which is easily rearranged as

$$\frac{T_{0(m)}}{T_{0(p)}} \cdot \frac{V_{0(m)}}{V_{0(p)}} = \frac{L_{0(m)}}{L_{0(p)}}.$$

This tells us any one of the three scale factors when the other two have been decided. In acoustic modelling it is not practically possible to have different velocities for the sound-waves in the model and in the prototype, so $V_{0(m)}/V_{0(p)}$ is 1. Our equation tells us that under these conditions time must be scaled down by the same factor as length—our earlier conclusion, but systematically deduced.

The scale of acceleration, like that of time, is related to the scales of length and of velocity. It can be found from the matching of the dimensionless numbers $\frac{a_0 L_0}{V_0^2}$ between model and prototype (see the fifth row of Figure 6(c)).

In problems where the acceleration due to gravity is a significant variable —as it is for models like that of Figure 4 in which the flow of water is produced by gravity—it is usually taken as the reference acceleration a_0.

The number $\frac{a_0 L_0}{V_0^2}$ is then replaced by $\frac{g_0 L_0}{V_0^2}$. The reciprocal of this dimensionless quantity is sometimes called the Froude number.

In securing dynamic similarity many more dimensionless numbers may be involved in the determination of scales for various physical properties. As examples, for force, viscosity, surface tension and bulk modulus of elasticity we have (from Figure 6(c), or by inference from Table 2) $F_0/(\rho_0 L_0^2 V_0^2)$, $\mu_0/(\rho_0 L_0 V_0)$, $\sigma_0/(\rho_0 L_0 V_0^2)$ and $K_0/(\rho_0 V_0^2)$. The first of these is sometimes called the Newton number when F_0 is an aerodynamic force. The reciprocals of the other three are called the Reynolds number, the Weber number and the Cauchy number. The Cauchy number is the square of the Mach number, which you have probably heard of in the context of supersonic flight.

2.2.7 Realities of scale-modelling

The last few sections have described a systematic basis for scale-modelling. They have provided a clarification of what, exactly, we are trying to do when we resort to scale-modelling and a systematic approach to the relationships between scaling factors. You may have concluded that, armed with this theory, we can adopt scale-modelling as a means for the solution of any problem in engineering, confident that our system of rules will see us through. If so, you are wrong. The realities of the matter are best explained by an example, so once again we will turn to our ship on an infinite ocean.

A necessity in deciding what engines a ship should have is a good idea of the force that will be needed to propel the ship. This is one reason why scale-models of ships are built and tested, and is the one we shall attend to. The force in question is that needed to overcome the resistance to the motion of the ship. It is the dependent variable in the problem, the aspect of the ship's behaviour that the model is to predict.

The independent variables are the factors upon which the resistance to the ship's motion depends. They may be expected to include the shape, length and speed of the ship, its depth of immersion in the water and the roughness of its hull. The relevant properties of the water may include its density, its surface tension and its viscosity. Another important factor will be the acceleration due to gravity, because gravity has a major influence on the form of the free surface of water and hence on the formation of waves—you could say that a ship has to lift water out of its way against the force of gravity.

If a model is to be made dynamically similar to the moving ship the first step is to secure geometric similarity. Making a model hull with the same proportions as the ship's and arranging for the properly scaled depth of immersion present no inordinate difficulty. However, the requirement of geometrical similarity also includes the fine texture of the hulls—the barnacles on the ship's bottom, for instance—and the roughness of a ship's hull varies as the ship ages or is cleaned. Moreover, it is not easy to characterize roughness.

Greater difficulties appear when the question of complete dynamic similarity is broached. The consideration of surface tension, viscosity and gravity requires the matching, between model and prototype, of the Weber, Reynolds and Froude numbers. Let us consider the Froude number first. Similarity requires that $\frac{g_0 L_0}{V_0^2}$ have the same value for both model and prototype. It is not possible to arrange for the testing of the model in a gravitational field differing from that at the surface of the earth, so the values of $\frac{L_0}{V_0^2}$ must be made to match. This means that the scales of length and velocity must be related by

$$\left(\frac{L_{0(m)}}{L_{0(p)}}\right) = \left(\frac{V_{0(m)}}{V_{0(p)}}\right)^2. \qquad \textit{(Check this for yourself.)}$$

The equality of Reynolds numbers means that $\frac{\mu_0}{\rho_0 L_0 V_0}$ must have the same value in model and prototype, but if the model ship is to be tested in water, μ_0 and ρ_0 will have the same values for both. Hence $L_0 V_0$ must be the same for the model and the prototype, which means that

$$\left(\frac{L_{0(m)}}{L_{0(p)}}\right) \cdot \left(\frac{V_{0(m)}}{V_{0(p)}}\right) = 1,$$

and sets a second condition to be satisfied by the scales of length and velocity.

The two conditions we have derived only admit one possibility—that the model must be of the same absolute size as the ship and must travel at the same speed. This is not, you must agree, an encouraging prospect for the designer of a supertanker. Efforts to avoid this conclusion by finding a special liquid for which the quantity $\frac{\mu}{\rho}$ (which is sometimes represented by v and called the kinematic viscosity) differs substantially from that for water have not been successful.

To go on to consider the equality of Weber numbers is pointless. To secure complete dynamic similarity with a model of reasonable size is impossible. Some kind of incomplete dynamic similarity must suffice.

The first simplification is to jettison the Weber number, which is equivalent to ignoring the effect of surface tension. This is a very reasonable step to take: although a sewing needle placed carefully on the surface of still water can be supported by surface tension, a steel knitting-needle cannot. Surface tension has truly negligible effects on other than very small objects.

Were it also possible to neglect either viscous or gravitational effects all would be well. In many problems a single dimensionless number is the only significant independent variable, but the resistance of a ship is not so simple.

What is in fact done is to proceed on the *assumption* that the total resistance of the ship is the sum of two forces, one depending only on the Reynolds number and the other only on the Froude number. Viscous and gravitational effects are thus supposed not to interact in any way. The supposition embodies the idea that the viscous resistance is due mainly to the frictional drag on the water adhering to the surface of the hull while the resistance arising from gravitational influences has to do with the ship pushing the water aside, creating waves as it does so. The total resistance is thus conceived as made up from what are called the resistance due to skin-friction and the wave-making resistance.

A further assumption, to the effect that the skin-friction does not depend on the detailed shape of a ship's hull, allows the resistance due to skin-friction to be estimated from the results of tests made by dragging thin flat plates through water without producing waves. Such tests and calculations can be carried out for both model and prototype ships. Indeed, this time luck is on the designer's side because the tests can be made with plates of the actual materials to be used in both prototype and model; this means that the awkward matter of roughness can be disposed of.

Now a model ship is built to a convenient scale of length and is tested at a speed given by the scale of velocity that is found by matching only the Froude number to that of the prototype. When its estimated resistance due to skin-friction is subtracted from its measured total resistance the force constituting the wave-making resistance of the model is found.

> *Exercise*
> Find the scale of velocities if the scale of length is 1:64.

If
$$\frac{g_{0(m)}L_{0(m)}}{V_{0(m)}^2} = \frac{g_{0(p)}L_{0(p)}}{V_{0(p)}^2}$$
then
$$\left(\frac{g_{0(m)}}{g_{0(p)}}\right) \cdot \left(\frac{L_{0(m)}}{L_{0(p)}}\right) = \left(\frac{V_{0(m)}}{V_{0(p)}}\right)^2;$$
putting $g_{0(m)}/g_{0(p)} = 1$ and $L_{0(m)}/L_{0(p)} = \frac{1}{64}$ gives
$$\frac{V_{0(m)}}{V_{0(p)}} = \sqrt{\frac{1}{64}} = \frac{1}{8}.$$

The wave-making resistance is taken as the reference force in the model and in the prototype. The equality of their Froude numbers implies that they have *wave-making* similarity, so the dimensionless number $F_0/(\rho_0 L_0^2 V_0^2)$ will have the same value for each. This provides the scale-factor for wave-making forces and the wave-making resistance of the prototype can be found by scaling up that of the model.

> *Exercise*
> Find the scale-factor for wave-making forces if the scales of length and velocity are as in the previous exercise.

From
$$\frac{F_{0(m)}}{\rho_{0(m)}L_{0(m)}^2 V_{0(m)}^2} = \frac{F_{0(p)}}{\rho_{0(p)}L_{0(p)}^2 V_{0(p)}^2}$$
we have
$$\frac{F_{0(m)}}{F_{0(p)}} = \left(\frac{\rho_{0(m)}}{\rho_{0(p)}}\right)\left(\frac{L_{0(m)}}{L_{0(p)}}\right)^2\left(\frac{V_{0(m)}}{V_{0(p)}}\right)^2$$
$$= 1 \cdot \left(\tfrac{1}{64}\right)^2 \cdot \left(\tfrac{1}{8}\right)^2$$
$$= 1/262144.$$

The total resistance to the ship's motion is found by adding the calculated estimate of its resistance due to skin-friction to the wave-making resistance found from the results of the test on the model.

In selecting a scale of length, and in some details of testing, there is need for caution. Though the effects of surface tension may be negligible for the prototype—which is large—the omission of the Weber number from considerations of similarity may allow these effects to assume significance should the model be made too small. (A little boat can be propelled in a bath by a very weak solution of detergent allowed to drip from its stern, reducing the surface tension behind it.) Moreover, the assumption made very early on for the prototype, of very deep water and very remote shores, must be reflected in the relative sizes of the model and the tank in which it is tested. Matters like this, that set limits on the practical choice of scales, are called scale effects.

This procedure for finding the resistance to the motion of a ship is based on assumptions about the physical nature of the resistance. It is justified only if it works well enough. It was devised by William Froude in about 1870 and its success is reflected in the name of the Froude number.

This section is not intended to teach you how to design ships. It is to illustrate the way in which special techniques of modelling may have to be developed in particular branches of technology. In the modelling of rivers and estuaries the scale effects of surface tension make it necessary to develop ways of using distorted models; in acoustic modelling special methods are needed for modelling sound-absorbing materials; aeronautical engineers must develop methods to avoid the necessity for impossibly high speeds in wind-tunnels or for models bigger than their prototypes. When I said, right at the beginning, that in scale-modelling we need to know what matters but not how or why I was, therefore, oversimplifying. The business of scale-modelling demands of its practitioner enough insight into the how and why of phenomena to preserve him from scale effects and deliver him from the often too restrictive implications of the theory of similarity.

Section 3

Linear programming—a model from operational research

All the models that we have so far looked at in any detail were models of physical prototypes like clay pigeons, chemical compounds, or concert halls. Operational research, in contrast, is concerned to model activities and their effects—its business is to develop models that can help in the planning of activities that are directed at achieving some sort of goal.

3.1 The blending problem

To illustrate this sort of modelling I have chosen a rather simplified example of what is called the 'blending' problem. Suppose that a firm has to decide upon a mixture of ingredients for a canned dog food. The ingredients have the composition and costs that are set out in Table 3. The goal is the cheapest blend of those ingredients that complies with certain nutritional standards. The standards are set out in the lower part of the table.

Table 3

	Bean-meal	Meat-meal	Cereal
% Protein	50	50	0
% Fat	25	10	0
% Carbohydrate	15	0	90
% Indigestible fibre and ash	10	40	10
Cost (£ per ton)	60	50	40

Protein must be not less than 25% ⎫
Fat must be not less than 10% ⎬ in the blend
Indigestible matter must not exceed 20% ⎭

We can feel our way to a solution by first letting b, m and c represent the proportions in which the bean-meal, meat-meal and cereal are present in the blend. If we settle the values of two of these—b and m, say—the third one is fixed automatically because the three ingredients together make up the whole mixture, so

$$b + m + c = 1 \qquad (1)$$

or

$$c = 1 - m - b \qquad (2)$$

The cost of 1 ton of the blend is itself a blend of the costs of the ingredients in the proportions b, m and c. If we call the cost C, then

$$C = 60b + 50m + 40c. \qquad (3)$$

We can express this cost in terms of b and m only. Using equation (2) to substitute for c we have

$$C = 60b + 50m + 40(1 - b - m)$$

or, more concisely,

$$C = 20b + 10m + 40. \tag{4}$$

What is required is to choose b and m, each of them a positive fraction, so as to make the cost per ton, C, as low as possible. However, the choice is not an entirely free one; it is constrained, firstly by the standards imposed in Table 3 and secondly by an implication of equation (2).

Equation (2) implies that $(m + b)$ must not exceed 1. You cannot mix meat-meal and bean-meal and extract cereal from the resulting mixture, so c cannot be less than zero. We can write this condition as*

$$b + m \leq 1. \tag{5}$$

The next condition arises from the specification of protein content in Table 3. The amount of protein in one ton of the blend will be 50% of b tons from the bean-meal, 50% of m tons from the meat-meal, and none from the cereal. This total amount of protein must be not less than 25% of one ton, so

$$50b + 50m \geq 25. \tag{6}$$

Exercise

Find the condition imposed by the specification of fat content in Table 3.

Solution

$$25b + 10m \geq 10 \tag{7}$$

The requirement with regard to indigestible fibre and ash is a little more awkward to express in terms of b and m. In terms of b, m and c it is straightforward:

$$10b + 40m + 10c \leq 20.$$

To get rid of c, we can use equation (2), obtaining

$$10b + 40m + 10(1 - b - m) \leq 20$$

or working out the bracket,

$$10b + 40m + 10 - 10b - 10m \leq 20.$$

The terms in b cancel, and when we subtract 10 from each side of the condition we end up with

$$30m \leq 10$$

or

$$m \leq \tfrac{1}{3}. \tag{8}$$

Now we can state the problem as follows.

Find positive values of b and m that conform to all the conditions

$$m + b \leq 1 \tag{5}$$

$$50m + 50b \geq 25 \tag{6}$$

$$10m + 25b \geq 10 \tag{7}$$

$$m \leq \tfrac{1}{3} \tag{8}$$

while at the same time giving the least possible value for

$$C = 20b + 10m + 40. \tag{4}$$

* The sign $\leq$ is read as 'less than, or equal to' or 'not greater than'. The sign $\geq$ is read 'greater than, or equal to'. Relations containing these signs are called 'inequalities'.

It is certainly not obvious that such a pair of values (b, m) even exist. It may be impossible to comply with all the constraints (5), (6), (7) and (8) simultaneously. We can use a graphical analogy to find out. Let us look, for example, at the inequality (6). We can first divide both sides by 50 to get

$$m + b \geq \tfrac{1}{2}. \tag{9}$$

Now the axes of the chart in Figure 8a are scales for b and m. Any point on the chart thus corresponds to a pair of values (b, m). For some points the inequality (9) will be satisfied while for others it will not. The line

$$m + b = \tfrac{1}{2}$$

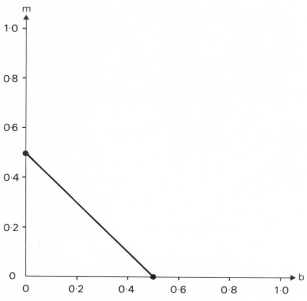

Figure 8a   Chart of m and b, showing the line $m + b = \tfrac{1}{2}$.

Figure 8b   Chart for completion.

has been plotted on the chart. If you check you will find that for any point on the same side of this line as the origin the condition (9) is broken, while for points on the line or to the other side of it the condition is satisfied.

In a similar way each of the conditions (5), (6), (7) and (8) states that acceptable values of b and m must correspond to a point that lies on, or to one side of, a particular line. An easy way to check the consistency of the conditions is therefore to draw the line for each condition in turn and shade that area of the chart that the condition rejects. Any unshaded area left after this has been done for all the conditions contains points whose co-ordinates, b and m, satisfy all the conditions.

Exercise

On Figure 8b draw the lines and shade the rejected areas corresponding to all the conditions (5), (6), (7) and (8).

Hint An easy way to locate the line for any particular condition is as follows. First replace the inequality sign by $=$, then put $b = 0$ and find the resulting value of m; plot this *on* the axis of m. Next put $m = 0$, find b and plot this on the axis of b. Join the two points you have plotted. Now go back to the original inequality and test to see if it holds when $m = b = 0$. If the condition is satisfied, shade the region on the side of the line away from the origin, if the condition is broken, shade the region on the same side as the origin. (This method doesn't work for condition (8) but that condition is more easily dealt with.)

The area **ABCDE** contains all the points whose co-ordinates, b and m, comply with all the conditions of the problem. This area is called the region of *feasible* solutions. Had the conditions been incompatible no such unshaded region would have existed. The problem would then have been insoluble. The result for the dog food manufacturer would have meant his

Solution
The solution of the exercise is given in Figure 9 in which strips have also been shaded to represent the conditions $m \geq 0$ and $b \geq 0$.

25

seeking further ingredients. However, the problem does have feasible solutions and in the area **ABCDE** there is a wide range of choice. It is the extent of this choice that leaves room for the seeking of the *optimal* or best solution, which in this case means the cheapest.

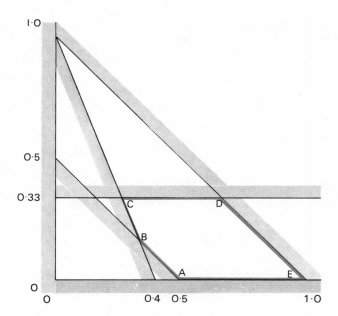

Figure 9   The region of feasible solutions for the blending problem.

The chart of Figure 9 provides us with a very simple process for finding the cheapest mixture. The cost per ton of blended ingredients we found to be

$$C = 20b + 10m + 40 \tag{4}$$

which we can re-arrange as

$$m = -2b + \left(\frac{C}{10} - 4\right). \tag{9}$$

If a particular cost is chosen, say £50 per ton, we can put $C = 50$ in equation (9) and find

$$m = -2b + 1. \tag{10}$$

This is the equation of a straight line on our chart. All the mixtures for which b and m satisfy this equation are represented by the points on this line, and all these mixtures are ones that would cost £50 per ton. The line is shown in Figure 8. Repeating the process for a cost of £45 per ton gives another line, also shown in the figure, with the equation

$$m = -2b + 0.5. \tag{11}$$

Any choice of C will give such a line, and every line of this kind will have the same slope, that is, -2. These lines are contours of cost in Figure 10. You can see that the cost increases steadily as these contours get further and further from the origin. The cheapest possible blend is given by the values of b and m for the point **B** in the feasible region because this is the first acceptable point that a line of slope -2 will strike as it slides away from the origin.

In our example, then, the optimal mixture is picked out by the red line. It is one-third bean-meal, one-sixth meat-meal and one-half cereal. Its cost is £48$\frac{1}{3}$ per ton. These results can be found from equations (2) and (4) when b and m have been got either by measurement from the chart or by solving simultaneously the equations of the two lines **AB** and **CB**.

26

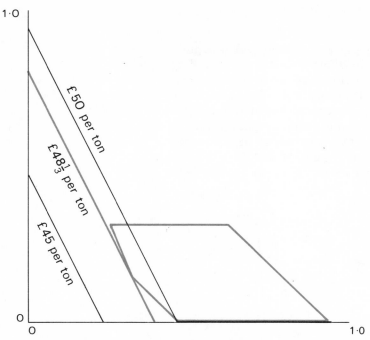

Figure 10   Cost contours and the feasible region for the blending problem.

Exercise

In the example of the dog food what mixture would be optimal, and what would it cost per ton if the price of cereal were to rise to £45 per ton?

3.2   Linear programming

The blending problem was modelled, as you just saw, by an algebraic problem: to choose the values of some variables (in the example, the proportions of the blend) in such a way as to satisfy a set of constraints and at the same time to provide an optimal value (in the example, the least possible value) of some clearly defined quantity (in the example, the cost). This form of algebraic problem turns out to be a symbolic model of a remarkably large variety of planning problems. The optimum sought may be a minimum, as it was in our example, or a maximum, as it might have been had the example been based on the manufacturer's profits rather than his costs. The quantity to be optimized is called the objective-function or the functional or one of many other possible names. When the functional and the constraints take the form that they took in the example, they are called linear (all our drawing involved only straight lines) and the problem is called a problem in linear programming.

The example that we have looked at is not typical of linear programming problems. We were able to get the solution by a graphical method because there were only two variables, b and m, to be found. Had there been four ingredients to be mixed three of the proportions would have had to be determined in order to fix the fourth. Instead of a flat drawing we would have needed a solid model with three axes to represent the three variable proportions. In three dimensions the feasible region would look rather like a cut gemstone. The contours of the objective function would be parallel plane surfaces. With five ingredients, and hence four independent variables, we cannot visualize a suitable geometrical model. However, the notion of the feasible region crossed by contours of the objective function can still be used as the basis for an algorithm applicable to any finite number of variables and constraints. In practice the limitation on the size of the problem—that is, on the numbers of variables and constraints—is set only by the size of digital computer that is available.

Solution

The feasible region is unchanged by the change in the price of cereal. The cost of a blend becomes

$C = 60b + 50m + 45c$

$\quad = 60b + 50m + 45(1 - b - m)$

$\quad = 15b + 5m + 45$

Therefore

$$m = -3b + \left(\frac{C}{5} - 9\right) \text{ for a fixed cost.}$$

The cost-contours thus have the slope -3. If a line of slope -3 is slid out from the origin it first reaches the feasible region at **C**. At **C** m is $\frac{1}{3}$ and b is $\frac{4}{15}$. These lead to $c = \frac{2}{5}$, $C = £50\frac{2}{3}$ per ton. In decimals this solution is $m = 0.333$, $b = 0.267$, $c = 0.400$, $C = £50·667$ per ton.

3.3 Mathematical programming

The name mathematical programming is given to the entire class of problems in which an objective function is to be maximized or minimized by the choice of some variables that are subject to constraints. Such problems can still be thought of in terms of feasible regions and contours, but in the general case the feasible region may have curved boundaries, and the contours of the objective function may also be more complicated than in linear programming. If there are only two variables to be chosen the graphical approach is still possible and Figures 11 and 12 give some indication of the complications that can arise.

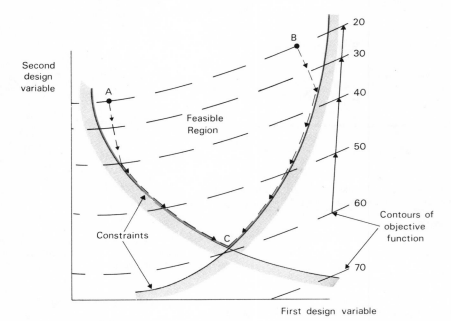

Figure 11   *A non-linear programming problem.*

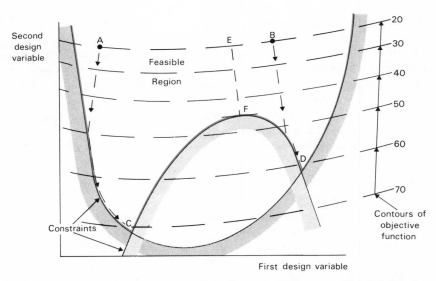

Figure 12   *A non-linear programming problem, showing how a concavity of the feasible region can give rise to a sub-optimum.*

In Figure 11 the boundaries of the feasible region are curved and the contours of the objective function are curved. The objective function clearly has its greatest value at *C*. In mathematical programming the usual algorithm for finding a maximum of the objective function is to proceed by short steps, from the best point so far found, in the direction of steepest increase (or decrease) of the objective function, but staying always within the feasible region. In Figure 11 paths of this sort are shown from *A* and *B*. Both of them arrive safely at *C*.

Things are less straightforward in Figure 12. The real optimum is at *C*, and is reached by the path from *A*. But from *B* the path of steepest ascent leads to *D*. In fact any path from a point to the right of the line *EF* will, if it always proceeds in the direction of greatest immediate improvement, end up at the *sub-optimum D*. In this two-dimensional case it is easy to distinguish the optimum from the sub-optimum, but this is not so readily done when there are several variables in the problem.

The critical distinction between Figures 11 and 12 is that in Figure 11 the feasible region is convex—any line joining two points of the region lies entirely within the region—and the objective function is also convex—if any two points are chosen, the value of the objective function at the point mid-way between them is not less than the average of the values at the two chosen points. In these circumstances there can be no sub-optimum. In Figure 12 the sub-optimum occurs because the feasible region is not convex. If it were, the line *DC* would have to be within the region, and a rising path could be followed from *D* to *C*.

My reason in making these general remarks about mathematical programming is that many writers use the general problem of mathematical programming as a parallel, often only metaphorical, of engineering design. The choices open to the designer are represented as the variables of the programming problem. Legal constraints, safety requirements and so on define the boundaries of the feasible region, and the objective function is usually cost (to be minimized) or profit (to be maximized) although efforts are sometimes made to construct an objective function that embodies a number of criteria, each with some chosen weighting.

Models and the designer

In Modelling 1, I explained that models are developed in science for their own sake, or rather, for the sake of understanding the phenomena of the natural world. The technologist's main interest in models is quite different. In general he wants models to help him in designing. One way of making this distinction is to say that for the scientist the prototype comes before the model, as some aspect of, or phenomenon in, the natural world, whereas for the technologist the model comes before the prototype. This distinction is helpful in contrasting science and technology, but too great an emphasis on the contrast would be misleading. There is no doubt that scientists often seek an understanding of phenomena with the underlying idea of bringing those phenomena within the reach of design; and one of the greatest arts of science is actually one of design—the design of experiments, which frequently involves the design of the necessary equipment. Technologists may also function, in the above sense, as scientists; very often there is a lack of knowledge of a general and scientific kind about phenomena relevant to some whole group of design problems, and the development of models for the understanding of these phenomena is undertaken by technologists. The matter simply reduces to the way we apply the labels 'scientist' and 'technologist'.

If a model gives a faithful representation of its prototype then it is a good model, a valid model. You will remember from Modelling 1 that it is not easy to be sure about the validity of a model. The procedure used in science is to use the model to make a prediction about the behaviour of the prototype and then to compare this prediction with actual behaviour in an experiment. To get the most effective results a scientist will try hard to test some aspect of the prototype's behaviour that would be very unlikely to occur if the model was not valid—that is, a point of behaviour that depends critically upon the details of the model. Then, if the model is faulty, it is found to be faulty as soon as possible and a better model can be sought.

Because all models misrepresent their prototypes to some extent (for example the phenomena of friction are left out of most models in mechanics) and because measurements can never be made exactly, the observed behaviour of the prototype seldom corresponds exactly with the predictions even of a very good model. There are thus models having different degrees of accuracy, which range from very good to very rough. Often a model is very good under some conditions and very bad under others. For example, the model we developed in Modelling 1 of the relationship between the pressure, volume and temperature of a mass of gas is very good if the temperature is high enough. At temperatures approaching those at which the gas could condense as a liquid, the model is less accurate, its accuracy deteriorating with decreasing temperature until, rather than calling the model inaccurate, we would call it invalid and look for a different one. The essential idea here is that a model has a range of validity, or accuracy. Usually models are accurate over a limited range of conditions; the simpler the model the more limited its range tends to be. The process of checking the validity of models—testing ideas to destruction —is the basis of scientific method.

I want now to focus attention on the use of models in design, which I take to be a major function of technology. The usual starting point for a designer is a description of the behaviour he is to produce in whatever it is he is designing. This description constitutes a more or less detailed specification, and determines, largely, what is to be taken as relevant to the behaviour (or performance) of the prototype. The specification sets limits of acceptable performance. The process of design consists in choosing what to put together, in what way, in order to obtain a performance that satisfies the specification.

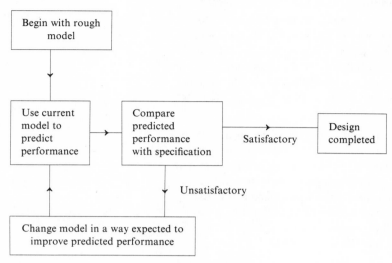

Figure 13   *A crude model of the process of design.*

Figure 13 shows, in a very simplified manner, the role of the technologist's model in design. Despite its formalized appearance this figure is a very vague description of design. It will, however, serve as a basis for discussing the abilities a technologist must exercise in using a model and the sort of model that he needs.

The vague exhortation 'Begin with a rough model' implies that the designer must have some sort of IDENTIKIT for modelling. This basic equipment comprises a range of general models drawn from science and from the designer's past experience. The better a designer is, the fewer times he will have to work his way around the loop.

In using the model to predict performance the designer may need logical or mathematical or computing techniques; he may use graphical models or scale-models, but because scale-models are expensive they are unlikely to be used at an early stage in design. In general the design is developed with models of increasing detail and complexity in successive passages around the loop of Figure 13.

In any but the simplest designs it is much easier to say 'Change the model to improve the predicted performance' than to say how this is to be done. The making of predictions from a given model is called analysis; it is comparatively easy to formalize and to teach. The step of assembling the model is called synthesis; it is the real art of the designer and is very difficult to teach because it cannot be formalized.

It is in the comparing of the performance predicted by the model with a specification that what a technologist wants from his model differs most significantly from what a scientist wants from his. The scientist's requirements are generality and accuracy. A designer, at least when he is designing, has no urge for generality, and the sort of accuracy that interests him is quite different from the scientist's.

It is probably true (I can think of no exceptions) that specifications for design always include multiple conditions of acceptability. (Imagine describing to somebody something you wanted them to make for you.) The designer's interest is in the answers to a series of questions about the design—does it satisfy each of the conditions of acceptability? These have answers of the kind 'Yes', 'No', or 'Very probably', and the designer's model has essentially to provide him with a reasonable measure of confidence in answering in this way. He may thus often be satisfied with a very simplified model; he does not demand accuracy if he can be sure that any inaccuracies are on the side of prudence. To use a more intricate model than the specification warrants is a waste of his time and resources. What constitutes a valid model for a technologist may thus differ considerably from what a scientist would want. An extreme example of this occurs in designs involving steel structures. One way of establishing that a structure will not collapse under a given loading depends not on finding out exactly how the structure would resist the load but merely on showing that there is at least one way in which it *could* resist the load. This allows the designer to answer the 'Yes' or 'No' question that interests him, but gives no other information at all.

What prompts a designer to use more and more accurate models is the prospect of greater economy of design. When more elaborate models are used the costs of design are increased in order to save on the eventual product. The nature of the product is thus another factor in determining the designer's model. If the product is to be mass-produced a tiny saving on each item can justify a large investment of the designer's time. Similarly if the design is for a huge project the prospects of very large savings in materials make the use of elaborate models worthwhile.

In much civil engineering design the overriding criterion of acceptability is safety. The designer is fairly content to use a 'factor of ignorance'—that is to provide what is probably excessive strength in a structure by a margin sufficient to cover any inaccuracy in the models he uses. In contrast an aircraft-designer must use more refined models, balancing the requirement of safety against those of payload, range, cruising speed and fuel-consumption.

Another feature of modelling in design is that technologists must often rush in where scientists fear to tread. It is unfortunate but nevertheless true that many commonplace things like rivetted or welded joints in steel, piled foundations for bridges or buildings, the rocks through which tunnels are driven and innumerable others, are so complex in their behaviour that no detailed models for them have ever been devised. Things like these must somehow be dealt with by designers, and many engineering models that have been developed for such purposes are described in the professional literature and Codes of Practice. These models often take the form of lists of conditions compliance with which has been found to constitute a guarantee against failure. These checklists summarize experience gathered from practice and from tests carried out, often at full-scale, in engineering research stations and universities. It is most unlikely that the need for models of this sort will ever diminish.*

* You may find it interesting to compare this sort of model with the one in Figure 10 of Modelling I.

Section 5

Technological progress and the availability of models

'Progress' is a dangerous word. Like 'justice', 'democracy', and 'wicked' one of its principal uses is in smuggling prejudice into an argument under the guise of objectivity. It is just a hurray-word, and anybody using it should be asked at once by what criterion he wishes to distinguish an arbitrary change from a progressive one. If such a criterion is agreed upon it is then important that no more significance be attached to the word 'progress' than that criterion justifies. This having been said, it is quite easy to give a criterion of technological progress. In the last section I suggested that a central practice of technology is that of designing to meet a specification. Progress in technology can, then, be taken to be an increase of proficiency in designing to meet specifications, either by the development of easier methods for meeting existing kinds of specification or by the development of methods for meeting a greater range and variety of specifications. This definition says nothing at all about the desirability or otherwise of the ends specified. It is like saying that a sharp knife is better than a blunt one in that it can be used for a greater range of purposes.

The central role of modelling in the process of design makes it hardly necessary to remark that technological progress is conditional upon the development of models of natural phenomena. There are, of course, equally important conditions regarding the sort of component parts, or elements, that a designer can incorporate in his design. Charles Babbage was able to design an automatic computer, but unable to construct it; he was able to design each mechanical part, but unable to make it; he was working on the design of machines to make the necessary parts when he ran out of time. Thus, true though it may be that the availability of models is a necessary condition of technological progress, it is not in itself sufficient.

It is interesting and important, though, to observe how different degrees of ease in modelling bias the development of technology. Probably because of the simplicity of the systems with which they deal, physics and chemistry provide a large number of accurate models of natural phenomena. Most modern technology reflects the availability of these models and is thus concerned principally with the inanimate world.

Any question of relationships between technological progress and social progress naturally raises again the meaning of 'progress', this time in a social context. Here it is by no means easy to secure agreement as to a criterion of progress. Nevertheless attempts are being made to construct 'models' intended to help in the making of decisions in matters of social concern, and these 'models' are most likely to find application in decisions about technological projects such as motorways, airports and reservoirs. They go by the name of cost-benefit analysis. It is important to realise that these 'decision-models' are quite different from the models normally used by scientists and technologists, or even in most operational research. They have no prototype with whose behaviour their predictions can be compared.

Cost benefit studies derive their existence from a notion of optimality like that which you met in section 3 of this unit. They involve the construction of an objective-function by the assessment of the costs and benefits of projects, and the assumption that this can meaningfully be done in every problem involving a decision. In operational research this approach has been applied with considerable success, but this success merely reflects the simplicity of the commercial policies and values with which mathematical programming deals. It is widely argued that this simplicity is quite untypical of social goals and values.

To set up an objective-function all values must be expressed in the same terms, and money serves readily as a measure of things that are customarily bought and sold. Attempts to use money to gauge other sorts of value are usually supported by arguments to the effect that every man has his price, but no models of value-systems have ever been devised that have validity in the sense of commanding universal assent.

It is often assumed or implied that the only thing wrong with cost-benefit analysis is that we have not yet found the right objective-function. This view seems to embody a belief in the existence of some prototype whose form is known but whose details have yet to be discovered. But a decision to use cost-benefit analysis is a matter of policy, not of fact, and every assumption needed to assign a monetary value to something that is not usually valued in this way is an additional policy decision. Moreover these are very indirect approaches to policy—they amount to rules about the way decisions are to be made but specify no actual goal of policy. For example, the nutritional conditions in the blending problem of section 3 were examples of absolute constraints. It could be claimed that to specify conditions in this way is to put an infinite value on nutritional standards; such claims are often made in arguments about cost-benefit analysis and whether or not money is the measure of all things. Now, instead of making the relevant nutritional standards absolutely rigid it would have been possible to change the cost-function whose value was to be minimized. Penalty costs could have been added which increased with the amount by which a blend departed from the nutritional standards.

In this way those boundaries of the feasible region that were set by nutritional standards would disappear, but the contours of the cost-function would no longer be straight lines. If the penalties were very large the likelihood of a blend being chosen much outside the previous feasible area would be small. (This is a representation of the way that absolute limits in quality can be enforced by the imposition of fines.) But if the penalties were not very heavy it would be impossible to foresee the outcome should the costs of ingredients begin to vary. This example shows the logical difference between the uses of absolute constraints and of weighted objective functions. The first course of action does provide for the maintenance of specific standards despite changes in the terms of trade. The second does not, unless the penalties (and thus, effectively, the monetary valuations of essentially non-economic standards) are so great that to distinguish them from absolute constraints is pointless.

If major decisions are based upon an accumulation of minor decisions whose interactions are not readily appreciated some very odd results can emerge, as the article in Appendix 1 shows. That the Government's decision on the siting of the third London airport was to ignore the majority report of the Roskill commission indicates a recognition of the kind of criticism formulated in the article.

There are numerous sources of contention about cost-benefit analysis, including its philosophical basis, its economic foundations, and the problems that arise in practice even when the deeper questions are disregarded. These matters cannot be dealt with within the confines of this unit. Our concern here is only to distinguish models that embody policy from those dealing with fact.

Appendix 1

(Reproduced with permission from the Institute of British Geographers from *Area* 1970, No. 2, pp. 1–9.)

Westminster: the fourth London airport?

John Adams, University College London

Traffic forecasts indicate that the number of passengers passing through London area airports annually will rise from 20 million in 1970 to over 200 million by the year 2000. On the basis of these predictions the British Airports Authority argues that London will soon need a third airport. However, although the greater London region apparently needs and wants greatly expanded air transport facilities, no particular part of the region wants the airport. This is easy to understand, for while the region as a whole would presumably benefit from an airport, most of the costs of noise, congestion, decline in property values and other social costs would be borne by the small part of the region in which the airport was located.

The strength of local protest succeeded in forcing the government to abandon its approval of a third London airport at Stansted. Anticipating equally vehement objections from other localities the government saw the need for a clearly impartial investigation. It was important that possible alternative sites should be objectively weighed, and be seen to be objectively weighed, so that the inevitable opposition to the final selection could be effectively disarmed. While local opposition might still be understandable it would be morally indefensible if it could be 'objectively' demonstrated that the selfish interests of a few were blocking the greater benefit of the majority. Hence the Roskill Commission was appointed in 1968 to conduct an enquiry into the location and timing of new airport facilities for the London region.

The Commission's research programme has had two main objectives: first, to make as comprehensive as possible a comparison of the costs and benefits relevant to each of the four sites it selected (Cublington, Foulness,

Figure 14   *"It's all right, they stop by parachute "* (With acknowledgments to *The Evening Standard*.)

Nuthampstead and Thurleigh), secondly, to assess when the Third London Airport should come into service. Although its objectives can be stated very simply they define a task of staggering complexity. Every activity that would be disrupted by a new airport has connections with other activities that would also be affected, and they in turn have connections, and so on in an almost endless chain. Estimating the multiplier effect of the disruption of individual activities is by itself a difficult task. Measuring this effect for the simultaneous disruption of a large number of activities and establishments such as farming, recreation, schools, industry and scientific and defence establishments is infinitely more difficult. Also, the scale of everything connected with the Third London Airport is enormous. It is estimated that 65,000 people will be employed and that a city as large as Bristol will develop near the airport. New roads and railways will be needed; thousands of acres of agricultural land will be consumed and as much as £73 million will be needed to shift defence installations that will be affected.

Clearly it would be impossible to consider everything. The Commission had, of necessity, to select a limited number of factors that it considered to be the most important and then to make a large number of simplifying assumptions about the way in which these factors are related to each other. The major factors selected by the Commission for inclusion in the study and the costs associated with them are summarized in Table 1.

Table 1

Estimates of the Costs and Benefits (in £ millions, 1968 prices discounted to 1975)*

	Cublington	Foulness	Nuthampstead	Thurleigh
1. Total net costs	2264·6	2385·2	2273·9	2266·3
2. Airspace movement	960·0	973·0	987·0	972·0
3. Passenger user costs	887·0	1041·0	868·0	889·0
4. Costs falling on local interests (including loss of residential amenity, disruption of schools, hospitals, industry, agriculture, recreation)	54·5	44·9	65·7	54·5†
5. Capital costs	288·8	252·7	284·7	288·3†
6. Costs directly attributable to noise	14·3	11·1	23·9	14·4†

* Discounting refers to the practice of converting all costs to a base year value by reducing future costs by 10% per year compounded annually.

† Items 4, 5 and 6 are not mutually exclusive. 4 includes some capital and noise costs.

The above table was compiled from tables 29:1, 29:3 and 29:5 of Volume VII.

The table reveals first, that the total costs associated with the construction and running of the Third London Airport are immense, over £2,200 million discounted to 1975; second, that this sum is completely dominated by two items, airspace movement and passenger user costs; and third, that the costs which fall on local interests, the costs which have aroused most of the public controversy, appear by comparison to be insignificant. Comparing Cublington, the lowest total cost site, with Foulness, the highest total cost site, we see that Cublington has higher capital costs, higher noise costs, and higher costs falling on local interests, and also that Foulness' amenity and capital cost advantages are dwarfed by Cublington's movement and user cost advantages.

In any study such as this the final outcome of the calculations will be greatly influenced by the simplifying assumptions on which they are based. When the outcome indicates that factors that are apparently of greatest public concern weigh so little in the balance, we can expect to find the explanation not only in the calculations but also, and perhaps predominantly, in the initial assumptions. The Roskill study because of its ambitious scope promises to become a standard reference in the field of cost-benefit analysis. It is therefore instructive to look closely at the problems and potential dangers associated with some of its assumptions.

Air and Surface Movement Costs

Looking first at the airspace movement costs, we see that although the absolute difference between the least cost and the highest cost sites is fairly large, £27 million, the relative difference between them is small, less than 2·7%. The report does not describe the way in which these costs were calculated but does explain that they are based on the route structures used by the consultants who evaluated the air traffic management problems. In their report the consultants note that these route structures have not been 'optimized' and state that any optimization could alter the route mileages and flying times (Vol. VIII, 2. 2, p. 10 and 56). Because of lack of time it was perhaps necessary to assume that these 'non-optimized' route structures reflect the comparative airspace movement costs of the different airport configurations being considered. But, where the maximum difference found between the systems is less than 2·7%, the crudeness of the assumptions raises serious doubts about whether Cublington's £27 million advantage should be considered *significant*.

The maximum difference between the surface movement costs and benefits is larger, £173 million, and the objections to the manner in which it was calculated are somewhat more complicated. In order to compare user costs for the various sites the research team first had to predict the amounts of traffic that would flow to the different airports from the various parts of the country. To do this they used the following model:

$$T_{ij} = \frac{O_i\, D_j\, F_{ij}}{\sum\limits_j D_j\, F_{ij}}.$$

Where:

T_{ij} = the number of trips between zone i and airport j.

O_i = the total number of trips generated in zone i (i.e. the various parts of England).

D_j = the total number of trips attracted to airport j.

F_{ij} = the cost or fraction of distance between i and j.

The model allocates passengers from regions i to airports j in direct proportion to the attractiveness of the airports, D_j, and in inverse proportion to distance from i to j. Using this model and an accessibility measure derived from it, the Commission calculated the volume of traffic generated and its total costs. It reasoned that the more efficient the configuration of airports, the greater would be the total amount of traffic generated by it, and that this additional traffic constituted a benefit that could be assigned to the more efficient system. According to this reasoning Cublington generated £154 million more 'benefits' than Foulness; this advantage in user costs is more than two and a half times greater than *all* the costs falling on local interests at any of the potential sites.

Local opposition groups unfamiliar with the jargon and the methods of traffic planners could be expected to feel quite helpless when confronted with a sum so large and calculated with such sophistication. What is not made clear in the report is that these 'generated benefits' are derived purely and simply from assumptions built into the model. Gravity models have been used with considerable success to *allocate* given amounts of traffic among alternative destinations, but their ability to estimate the total amount of traffic *generated* by a network configuration is completely unproven.

The above model could be called a 'loosely attraction constrained' model. O_i, D_j and F_{ij} are *inputs* to the model and must be provided by the programmer; T_{ij}, the number of trips between i and j, is the *output*. A recursive solution procedure is used which permits O_i, D_j and F_{ij} to vary within certain limits but the total amount of traffic generated by the system is $\sum O_i$. O_i is a function of the population, income and accessibility to airports, of the various zones of origin. Accessibility is calculated by:

$$\text{Accessibility of zone i} = \frac{\sum_j (D_j F_{ij})}{\sum_j D_j} \cdot$$

The calculation of the amount of traffic generated depends heavily both on the assumed capacities of the various airports, and on the assumption that the functional relationship between accessibility and traffic will remain constant, while the volume of traffic increases tenfold. The first assumption is arbitrary and the second may be seriously questioned.

It is not disputed that efficient transport systems tend to generate more traffic than inefficient ones, but the Commission presents no proof that the differences it finds are *significant*. An analogy might make the point clearer. Imagine that British Rail is trying to decide whether to route all London-Glasgow trains from Euston Station or Liverpool Street Station. Euston might be more accessible to more people in London than Liverpool Street and hence would be the most 'efficient' choice, but it is unlikely that routing all trains from Liverpool Street would significantly affect the numbers of people going from London to Glasgow.

Comparing the per capita transport costs for Cublington and Foulness, it can be estimated from the report (Tables 13:10, 13:15 and 13:18) that the Cublington system will be one shilling and five pence cheaper in 1991 and less than three shillings cheaper in the year 2000. Given that the average total cost of an air journey is well above £20 the possible savings would appear to amount to less than 0·5% of the total journey cost. It is highly unlikely that savings of this magnitude would have any perceptible effect on the total volume of traffic. Indeed elsewhere in the report the Commission considers the probable effect of a 6% increase in the journey cost and concludes that 'it can hardly be considered significant'. (Vol. VII, p. 105). Yet it is calculated in the report that the savings resulting from the selection of Cublington instead of Foulness would induce an additional 11 million people to fly and generate benefits of over £150 million.

Costing Amenity Losses

The Commission acknowledges that it is extremely difficult to attach monetary values to benefits that are not customarily appraised in these terms but argues that it is necessary in order to make a fair comparison among the alternative sites. It also states that the attempt to value non-material benefits in monetary terms in no way implies a materialistic view of life (Vol. VII, p. 6). This is a questionable assertion for it is very unlikely that it would occur to a non-materialistic society to consider the problem in this way. But what seems to me to be beyond question is that the values the Commission attaches to non-material benefits reveal a very strong bias which is not only materialistic and philistine but also discriminatory against low income groups.

This is particularly evident in its evaluation of recreational activities, churches, historic buildings, and residential amenities. For example, the cost assigned to the disruption of transferable recreational activities such as sightseeing and camping is simply the replacement cost of fixed facilities, if any, plus the additional time and travel costs of getting to an alternative site. If the activities associated with a site are considered unique and irreplaceable a price must still be attached to their loss. The report calculates this 'subjective' loss as the sum of what participants pay for an activity (admission fees and travel costs) plus any consumer surplus they enjoy. Consumer surplus is the difference between the price that participants actually pay and the price they would be prepared to pay if pushed to the limit. In practice this means that the value attached to a recreational site is simply the cost to the users of getting to it, plus their expenditure there, plus what they would be prepared to pay for the privilege of keeping it. But no matter how much someone may enjoy an activity, if it is free, and if he cannot afford to pay for it, then his loss if it is taken away has no cash value (Vol. VII, chap. 24).

The costing of churches is treated in the report in a similarly straightforward manner. It is argued that the payment of insurance premiums is a strong indication of the value placed on property and insurance values were accordingly used for the valuation of churches likely to be affected by the new airport. It recognized that this method did not fully take into account historic benefits but argued that such benefits are unlikely to be much greater than the insurance values. The obvious objection to this procedure is that insurance values must be related to market values or replacement costs. Since there is no market for the sale of old churches to collectors their market value is extremely small. Historic value is irreplaceable and quite unrelated to the cost of physically replacing a building (letters to *The Times*, 13 Feb., 1970).

In the summary table the cost of churches is included under the heading recreation. The total 'recreation' costs associated with the four sites are: Cublington—£6·7 million, Foulness—£0·3 million, Nuthampstead—£3·6 million, and Thurleigh—£3·8 million.

The values attached to the amenity losses that would be suffered by people living close to the potential sites reveal another interesting bias in the Commission's assumptions. The report states that the market value of house property represents not only the house itself but all the environmental advantages and disadvantages attaching to it. From this it is argued that the market value of a house very precisely reflects the value of the house as a totality and therefore the depreciation of real estate values will accurately measure the loss of amenity suffered (Vol. VII, p. 25).

This potential loss was estimated for residential property near the new airport sites by applying the depreciation rates found for similar property around Heathrow and Gatwick. It was found that depreciation was principally determined by three factors: noise levels associated with aircraft, general neighbourhood background noise levels, and the class of property. The higher the level of aircraft noise the greater was the depreciation suffered, but the higher the general background noise level the less was the effect of aircraft noise. However, of greater importance than either of the first two factors was property class. On average, for all noise levels, the percentage depreciation in value for high class property was four times the depreciation for low class property (Vol. VII, table 20.3). In other words, because their property values were little affected the poor were assumed, for quantifying purposes, to be little bothered, and small or nil values were attached to their amenity loss.

Benefits

Although the work is called a cost-benefit study it is mainly concerned with comparing the costs associated with alternative airport systems. The benefits mentioned so far have simply been the difference between the highest and least cost sites. But what are the benefits which justify the costs associated with the minimum cost site?

A fundamental assumption of the whole report is that London needs a new airport. Traffic, it is estimated, will reach 200 million by the year 2000 and traffic, it is assumed, is a benefit: 'To set against the net costs for each site there is what might be termed a 'base load' of benefits *not measured* (my italics) but for the existence of which it would be wrong to proceed with a third London airport at all' (Vol. VII. p. 103). If we extrapolate the forecasters' trends a few more years into the future this 'base load' of benefits becomes absolutely astounding. Over the past fifteen to twenty years air passenger traffic has been growing at a rate in excess of 10% per year and the forecasters saw no reason to expect a slower rate in the future. If we draw a graph of this 10% growth rate we see that traffic doubles approximately every seven and a half years. Such exponential growth rates very quickly produce absurdly high volumes of traffic. The Commission recognized that infinite growth was not possible and so decided that a ceiling would be reached when each business man made six trips per year and each non-business passenger made two trips per year. It admits that there is no evidence for such a ceiling, it simply assumes it to avoid the absurd alternative. However, this 'ceiling' is not reached until around the year 2000; during most of the thirty year forecast period traffic is assumed to increase exponentially.

The response of the Commission was to plan for these volumes as if they were some natural and inevitable phenomenon. However, unlike natural phenomena with exponential growth rates, air traffic has no realistic 'natural' physical limit at which it must ultimately level off. The limit is set by the facilities provided and the charge made for them. The experience of road traffic planners suggests that if travel continues to become cheaper and if roads are provided to accommodate an exponential growth rate, then traffic will continue to increase exponentially. At the present time those who fly are not charged for the privilege of disturbing those below. The Commission recognizes that this lack of compensation for loss of amenity could be considered a concealed subsidy for air travel, but argues that compared to the 'unmeasured base load of benefits' it is insignificant. Would it argue the same case in the year 2000?

Westminster Airport

The direction in which the Commission's assumptions are leading can be illustrated by repeating the exercise for the year 2000 by which time a fourth airport will be needed. If we add Westminster to the list of sites that might be considered and apply the Roskill cost-benefit criteria, what potential savings would be associated with a central London site? At a conservative estimate it would save one hour per journey plus the cost of ground transport. Given that a businessman's time in the year 2000 is valued at over £3·50 per hour and a tourist's time at over £·40 per hour we can very conservatively estimate the average savings at £1·50 per journey (constant prices are assumed throughout). Thus the savings in the year 2000 would be over £300 million per year and over the thirty year life of the airport would amount to £9000 million. It can be assumed that the annual increase in the number of passengers will cancel out the discount rate so that the total savings discounted to the year 2000 would be £9000 million.

Property values around Hyde Park are about £30 per square foot and drop to about £3 per square foot in Notting Hill. Valuing Hyde Park and Green Park and immediately adjacent land at the higher figure and additional land required at the lower figure it appears that a five square mile central London site could be purchased for about £2500 million. An additional seven square miles could be insulated against sound at £4 per square foot and its population generously compensated for depreciated property values for another £1000 million. Westminster Abbey could be insulated or moved and in any event would be unlikely to be worth much more than its insured value of £1·5 million. An additional £3000 million could be allowed for generous supplementary compensation and the total saving would still amount to £2750 million. These estimates, although admittedly rough, appear not unrealistic when compared with estimated cost of the London motorway system. The motorway scheme would require 20 square miles of land and displace between 60,000 and 120,000 people; its total cost, including construction costs, is estimated at between £1,100 and £2,200 million (Thompson, 1969, p. 130, 142).

The loss of the parks would represent a major amenity loss but this has been accounted for by the high values attached to the parkland and adjacent real estate. Also the airport itself would represent a major recreational amenity. It has been noted in the report that large numbers of people are attracted to Heathrow and Gatwick to watch the aircraft and listen to conversations between control tower and pilot.

The safety of those on the ground would appear to be an insignificant consideration. The report anticipates only one 'Third Party' accident over thirty years and the costs assumed are only £9300 for each fatality and £625 for each injury. These costs could of course be discounted along with all other future costs (Vol. VII, p. 309).

It is possible that the accounting assumptions found in the report are an accurate reflection of generally held values. This was certainly the intention of the Commission. If they are, then there would appear to be a strong prima facie case for including Hyde Park in the short list of sites to be considered for a fourth London Airport.

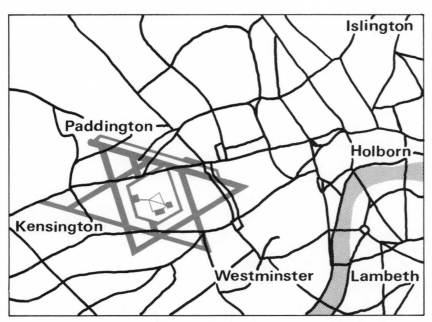

Figure 15   Proposed site for Westminster Airport. Heathrow runways superimposed on Hyde Park. (Crown Copyright Reserved.)

Conclusion

Advances in telecommunications are very rapidly reducing the effect of distance on the flow of information. Along with increased affluence and developments in transport technology they are stimulating greatly increased traffic in goods and people. Problems similar to those confronting the Roskill Commission can be expected to become more common. As population densities increase and people become more mobile it will become more and more difficult to provide adequate transport facilities without disturbing large numbers of people. As the scale of disruption grows larger the traditional ways of measuring its cost will become completely inadequate. The character of whole regions will be altered and the general public will be called upon to put a price on its way of life.

The Third London Airport will perform what is essentially a London function for which there is no room in central London. The benefits will accrue largely to London: the 'way of life costs' will fall entirely on the local region where the airport is located. The project thus implies a spatial redistribution of income. A cost-benefit analysis can be used to decide which site is cheapest from the point of view of transport costs, or construction costs, or land acquisition costs, or even church destruction costs. But it cannot decide whether saving millions of London passengers 5 minutes each justifies disrupting the way of life of mere thousands. That decision is not quantifiable.

References

Commission on the Third London Airport, 1970. Papers and Proceedings. Volumes VII and VIII, London.

Sealy, K. R., 1967. The Siting and Development of British Airports. *Geographical Journal*, 133, 148–77.

Thompson, J. M., 1969. *Motorways in London*, London.

Self-assessment questions and exercises

These questions, though numbered consecutively are sometimes named as SAQs and sometimes, when they involve subtleties that may well not be clear from a reading of the unit, Exercises.

SAQ 1

Here are definitions of several physical quantities:

(i) The stress, τ, on a surface is defined as the force per unit area of the surface.

(ii) The velocity gradient, $\dfrac{dV}{dx}$, in a fluid, is defined as the rate of change of velocity, V, with position, x.

(iii) The viscosity, μ, of a fluid is the shear stress per unit velocity gradient.

(iv) The stiffness, k, of a spring, is the force per unit extension of the spring.

(v) The force, F, required to move a body steadily through a fluid at a velocity V can often be expressed by a formula of the type

$$F = CV^n$$

where n is a dimensionless constant. C can be called the damping coefficient.

Find the dimensions of τ, $\dfrac{dV}{dx}$, μ, k and C in terms of $[M]$, $[L]$ and $[T]$.

SAQ 2

A mass M is attached to the free end of a spring of stiffness k. See what you can find out about the period, T, of vibration of the arrangement, by considering the dimensions of the physical quantities concerned.

Exercise 3

A pendulum is made by suspending a mass M at the free end of a weightless rigid rod of length l, at a place where the acceleration due to gravity is g. Use arguments based on dimensions to discuss the way in which the periodic time, T, of the pendulum depends on M, l, g and α, the angle the pendulum makes with the vertical when it is released.

What will be the effect on T when the mass is doubled?

What will be the effect on T if α is doubled?

Exercise 4

If the pendulum bob in Exercise 3 is subject to damping of the type mentioned in SAQ 1(v), with $n = 1$, then the coefficient C is a relevant physical variable. Find a set of dimensionless products in terms of which this extended problem could be investigated.

SAQ 5

Experiments to determine the curve shown in the solution to Exercise 3 are to be carried out by testing a pendulum in air. Does any difficulty with scale effects seem likely to arise? If so, what measures might be adopted to counter it?

SAQ 6

The blending problem of the text is to be repeated with a different objective-function. The dog-food is to be used in equipping an antarctic expedition and the overriding criterion is to store the food in the least possible space. The relative volumes of equal weights of the ingredients are bean-meal; meat-meal: cereal $= 1:1.1:1.3$. Determine the optimum blend and find the saving in storage space as compared with the cheapest blend.

The following question, although quite straightforward, will require about an hour's work for its solution.

SAQ 7

A chemical plant uses feedstocks of three materials, α, β and γ. According to the mixture of reactants and the arrangement of other controlling variables the running conditions can be optimized for any of three processes. The average hourly rates of consumption of α, β and γ and the average hourly outputs of three products X, Y and Z, all in tonne/hour are set out in the table below for each of the three processes, A, B and C.

The plant has standing orders, which must be complied with, equivalent to an average of 6 tonne/hour of X and 4 tonne/hour of Y. Any production of Z exceeding an hourly average of 5 tonne/hour is unsaleable. The waste-disposal arrangements cannot provide for an average rate of waste exceeding $2\frac{2}{3}$ tonne/hour from any process.

The materials α, β and γ cost, respectively, £4, £8 and £5 per tonne, while the products X, Y and Z can be sold at respective prices of £40, £50 and £20 per tonne. The remaining costs of production are fixed.

(i) Determine the most profitable way in which production time can be apportioned between the three processes; find the resulting mix of products X, Y and Z, and the profit per hour ignoring fixed costs.

(ii) What is the simplest measure that could be taken in order to increase the rate of profit?

Process		A	B	C
Average rates of consumption (tonne/hour)	α	4	8	4
	β	4	4	8
	γ	4	4	6
Average rates of production (tonne/hour)	X	8	4	3
	Y	2	8	2
	Z	–	–	12

Self-assessment answers

SAQ 1

(i) $[\tau] = \left[\dfrac{F}{A}\right] = \left[\dfrac{MLT^{-2}}{L^2}\right] = [ML^{-1}T^{-2}]$

(ii) $\left[\dfrac{dV}{dx}\right] = \dfrac{[dV]}{[dx]} = \dfrac{[V]}{[x]} = \left[\dfrac{LT^{-1}}{L}\right] = [T^{-1}]$

(iii) $[\mu] = \dfrac{[\tau]}{\left[\dfrac{dV}{dx}\right]} = \left[\dfrac{ML^{-1}T^{-2}}{T^{-1}}\right] = [ML^{-1}T^{-1}]$

(iv) $[k] = \left[\dfrac{F}{L}\right] = \left[\dfrac{MLT^{-2}}{L}\right] = [MT^{-2}]$

(v) $[C] = \left[\dfrac{F}{V^n}\right] = \left[\dfrac{MLT^{-2}}{L^nT^{-n}}\right] = [ML^{1-n}T^{n-2}]$

Notes

(a) The dimensions of force, area, and velocity are given in Table 1.

(b) In (ii) the infinitesimal increments dV and dx have the same dimensions as V and x respectively. Being infinitesimal does not change their dimensions.

(c) In (iii) the results of (i) and (ii) are used.

SAQ 2

From SAQ 1 the dimensions of k are $[MT^{-2}]$, while those of T and M are, obviously, $[T]$ and $[M]$. Since $[L]$ does not appear in the problem there are only two independent dimensions, $[M]$ and $[T]$. Buckingham's theorem tells us that the number of dimensionless products that can be involved in the answer is equal to the number of physical variables (three in this case—k, M and T) less the number of independent dimensions (two in this case). Hence there is only one dimensionless product to be found and it is easily worked out: the dimensions of k are $[MT^{-2}]$ so the dimensions of $\dfrac{k}{M}$ are $[T^{-2}]$, and so $\dfrac{kT^2}{M}$ is dimensionless.

Now Buckingham's theorem states that all physical relationships are between dimensionless products. Since there is only one product in this problem, the most that can be said about it is that it has a particular numerical value—let us call it b^2. Then

$$\dfrac{kT^2}{M} = b^2$$

or

$$T = b\sqrt{\dfrac{M}{k}}$$

and we know exactly the way in which M and k affect T. We do not, of course, know b. But one experiment will do to give us a value for b, and then we have a symbolic model valid for any mass on any spring.

A considerable amount of mathematics is needed to show that the theoretical value of b is 2π.

Exercise 3

In this problem there are five variables (M, l, g, T, α) and three independent dimensions ($[M]$, $[L]$ and $[T]$). There are, therefore, $5 - 3 = 2$ dimensionless quantities to be related to one another. The angle, α, is dimensionless and will serve as one of the two. The dimensions of g are $[LT^{-2}]$ so gT^2/l is dimensionless, and will serve as the second dimensionless product. Because M is the only one of the five physical quantities whose dimensions involve $[M]$, it *cannot* be combined with the others in any way that will give a dimensionless product. Hence it can appear in *no* relationship between dimensionless products, and so it can have *no effect* on the period.

We conclude that gT^2/l depends in some way on α, but either a sequence of experiments or a deeper mathematical analysis would be needed to obtain the details of the relationship.

The effect of doubling the mass is thus to leave the period unchanged, while the effect of doubling the angle from which the pendulum is released could only be ascertained from further investigation.

Exercise 4

The variables are M, l, T, g, α, C, six in all. There are three independent dimensions, so three dimensionless products are needed. Two of these can be taken as for Exercise 3, namely gT^2/l and α. The final one should include C.

The dimensions of C are from SAQ 1(v), $[MT^{-2}]$ when $n = 1$. Hence $\frac{C}{M}$ has dimensions $[T^{-2}]$. It is possible, therefore, to form the dimensionless product $\frac{CT^2}{M}$, but this is not very convenient because it contains T, which is our dependent variable. It is more useful to look for a different way of finding a quantity with dimensions $[T^2]$, by which to multiply $\frac{C}{M}$. We have $[g] = [LT^{-2}]$ so $\left[\frac{l}{g}\right] = [T^2]$. Hence $\frac{Cl}{Mg}$ is dimensionless, and will serve to characterize the damping. The three dimensionless products are thus $\frac{gT^2}{l}$, α and $\frac{Cl}{Mg}$.

Note: When the motion is damped the oscillations of the pendulum will die away. We cannot be sure that the time taken for a swing to the left and another back to the right will be the same for successive oscillations. We should therefore be prepared to add another variable, a whole number, m say, and use it to pick out the mth oscillation. As a number, m is, of course, dimensionless.

SAQ 5

The motion of a pendulum in air is bound to be damped. The proper description of the *experimental* circumstances should therefore be as in Exercise 4,* and should include C, the damping coefficient.† Scale effects due to the neglect of damping may therefore be expected to distort the graph based only on the dimensionless products gT^2/l and α. The third dimensionless product $\frac{Cl}{Mg}$ would be zero for $C = 0$, but if C cannot be made zero in the experiments (by testing in a vacuum, say) then at least $\frac{Cl}{Mg}$ can be made small by using a short pendulum (to get a small l) and a massive bob (to get a large M).

SAQ 6

Relative volume of blend $= V$, say, $= b + 1.1m + 1.3c$

$$\therefore V = b + 1.1m + 1.3(1 - b - m)$$

$$= 1.3 - 0.2m - 0.3b$$

Lines of constant volume have the slope -1.5 on the previous graph. The optimum is at **E**, where the relative volume is 1.0. At **B**, which gave the cheapest blend, the relative volume is, for $b = \frac{1}{3}$ and $m = \frac{1}{6}$,

$$V = 1.3 - \frac{1}{6} \times 0.2 - \frac{1}{3} \times 0.3$$

$$= 1.3 - 0.033 - 0.1$$

$$= 1.167$$

the saving in volume is thus 16.7%.

SAQ 7

Let the proportions of time allocated to the processes A, B and C be a, b and c. These must together make up all the operating time so,

$$a + b + c = 1 \qquad (1)$$

The average rate of production for X must be at least 6 tonne/h, so

$$8a + 4b + 3c \geq 6 \qquad (2)$$

The average rate for Y must be at least 4 tonne/h, so

$$2a + 8b + 2c \geq 4 \qquad (3)$$

The production of Z should not exceed 5 tonne/h, so

$$12c \leq 5 \qquad (4)$$

Under process A the combined hourly input of α, β and γ is 12 tonne and the combined useful output of X and Y is 10 tonne. The rate of waste is therefore 2 tonne/h. Process B creates waste at 4 tonne/h and process C at 1 tonne/h. The total rate of waste must not exceed $2\frac{2}{3}$ tonne/h so

$$2a + 4b + c \leq \frac{8}{3} \qquad (5)$$

If Equation (1) is used to express c as $1 - a - b$ the constraints on a and b become

$$a + b \leq 1 \qquad (1a)$$

$$5a + b \geq 3 \qquad (2a)$$

$$a + b \geq \frac{1}{3} \qquad (3a)$$

$$a + b \geq \frac{5}{12} \qquad (4a)$$

$$a + 3b \leq \frac{5}{3} \qquad (5a)$$

---

* In Exercise 4 the power, n, in the equation for the damping force is taken as 1, and this solution follows that assumption. Another choice of n could be dealt with in a parallel way but would give more complicated results.

† The damping force on a pendulum bob, given by the equation $F = CV^n$, depends upon the shape and surface area of the bob as well as its velocity and the properties of the fluid in which the bob is moving. The coefficient C must embody the effects of all these variable properties except the velocity. Thus C will be the same only for bobs of the same shape and size, moving in the same fluid. Bobs of the same shape and size can nevertheless differ in mass if their densities are different.

These inequalities define the feasible region on the chart below.

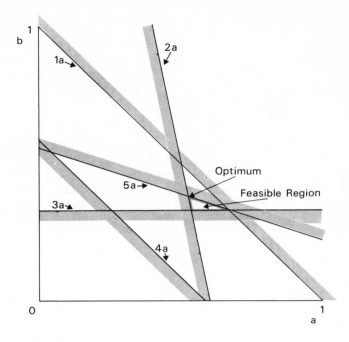

(i) The objective-function is the rate of profit, ignoring fixed costs. Process A involves hourly average costs of $4 \times £4 = £16$ for α, $4 \times £8 = £32$ for β and $4 \times £5 = £20$ for γ, a total of £68. Sales from this process amount to $8 \times £40$ for X and $2 \times £50$ for Y, totalling £420 per hour. The rate of profit is, therefore, $£420 - £68 = £352$ per hour. Similar calculations for processes B and C yield, respectively, £476/h and £350/h. The actual rate of profit, $£P$/h is given by

$$P = 352a + 476b + 350c$$

and when c is replaced by $1 - a - b$ this gives

$$P = 350 + 2a + 126b$$

Clearly the profit increases very rapidly with b, while a has little influence. Contours of profit are almost horizontal in the chart, and the optimum values of a and b can be read from the chart or found by solving the equations of the lines marked (2a) and (5a). This gives $a = \frac{11}{21}$, $b = \frac{8}{21}$, $c = \frac{2}{21}$. The rates of production are 6 tonne/h of X, $4\frac{2}{7}$ tonne/h of Y and $1\frac{1}{7}$ tonne/h of Z. The rate of profit, P, is $£399\frac{1}{21}$/h. I have given these answers as exact fractions, but decimal approximations within a couple of percent would result from measurement on the chart.

(ii) The two limitations operative at the optimum are those on the disposable waste and on the least admissible production of X. To arrange for the faster disposal of waste would allow the optimal point to move more rapidly in the direction of increasing profitability (up the line (2a)) but would involve some change in the fixed costs. On the other hand, an attempt to re-negotiate the standing order for X, at a value less than 6 tonne/h, would promise an immediate increase in profit, by allowing the optimum point to move to the left along the line (5a).